Picture History of the ITALIAN LINE 1932-1977

William H. Miller, Jr.

DOVER PUBLICATIONS, INC.
Mineola, New York

*For Maurizio Eliseo
and Paolo Piccione,
those exceptional "Italian boys"*

∼ ∼ ∼

Copyright

Copyright © 1999 by William H. Miller, Jr.
All rights reserved under Pan American and International Copyright Conventions.

Bibliographical Note

Picture History of the Italian Line, 1932–1977 is a new work, first published by Dover Publications, Inc., in 1999.

Library of Congress Cataloging-in-Publication Data

Miller, William H., 1948–
　Picture history of the Italian Line, 1932–1977 / William H. Miller, Jr.
　　p.　cm.
　Includes bibliographical references and index.
　ISBN 0-486-40489-7 (pbk.)
　1. Italian Line—History.　2. Italian Line—History Pictorial works.　3. Ocean liners—Italy—History. 4. Ocean liners—Italy—History Pictorial works.　5. Passenger ships—Italy—History.　6. Passenger ships—Italy—History Pictorial works.　7. Ocean travel—History.　8. Ocean travel—History Pictorial works.　I. Title.
HE945.I86M55　　1999
387.5'42'0945—dc21　　　　　　　　　　　　　　　　　　　　　　　　　　　　99-33035
　　　　　　　　　　　　　　　　　　　　　　　　　　　　　　　　　　　　　　CIP

Book design by Carol Belanger Grafton

Manufactured in the United States of America
Dover Publications, Inc., 31 East 2nd Street, Mineola, N.Y. 11501

Contents

Acknowledgements / PAGE VI
Foreword / PAGE VII
Picture Credits / PAGE VIII
Introduction / PAGE IX

∼ ∼ ∼

1. The Early Fleet / PAGE 1
2. Castles at Sea / PAGE 14
3. Classic Motor Liners / PAGE 20
4. To More Distant Shores / PAGE 26
5. Floating Palaces / PAGE 35
6. Rebirth and Restoration / PAGE 60
7. South American Sisters / PAGE 74
8. Other Italians, Other Routes / PAGE 83
9. Renaissance Ships / PAGE 98
10. The Italian Superliners / PAGE 118

∼ ∼ ∼

Bibliography / PAGE 131
Index / PAGE 133

Acknowledgments

The Italian Line archives are no more. Therefore, I am especially grateful to the ocean liner collectors, historians, and writers who have helped to create this photographic review of that Company's passenger fleet. For most of us, it would seem that there is never enough. Never enough of those evocative views of the liners at sea or berthed in port, those glorious views of their sumptuous interiors and those fascinating views of souls on board, the passengers and the crew members alike. Because of Dover and their great willingness to do ocean liner titles, these prized, often rare photos can be shared by many. We hope that it adds in some small way to the history of these great ocean liners.

I am immensely grateful to so many "ocean liner friends." Without their continued support, generosity and patience, there would not be books such as these. I am merely the organizer, the arranger, the catalyst. In a single afternoon, this particular project came much closer to reality. Paolo Piccione, a very fine Italian maritime historian and author, invited us for a visit to his Genoa apartment. Because of his exceptional generosity in loaning so many wonderful pictures, the idea of this book was firmly cemented. I am also indebted to another superb Italian ship expert, Maurizio Eliseo. Just as in the past, I also had great assistance (with photos as well as period brochures, deck plans, and sailing schedules) from that great passenger ship memorabilia dealer and expert, Richard Faber. I am also indebted to another splendid friend, Ernest Arroyo, who loaned many photos from the collection of the late Frank Cronican. Further special appreciation to Nicola Arena, Tom Greene, Sal Scannella, and Everett Viez.

Other photographers and photograph collectors who assisted include James Ciani, Alex Duncan, William Fox, Enrico Repetto, Victor Rollo, the late Roger Scozzafava, Antonio Scrimali, Roger Sherlock, and Gregory Vossos. Prized anecdotes and recollections came from the likes of Captain Raffaele Gavino, the late Vito Sardi, and Captain Mario Vespa. Companies and other organizations that assisted include Carnival Cruise Lines, Costa Line, Flying Camera Inc., Italian Line, Moran Towing & Transportation Company, and the Newport News Shipbuilding & Dry Dock Company.

And, of course, my warmest thanks go to my family and to Abe Michaelson, my business partner.

Foreword

The Italian Line was one of my favorite passenger lines. They had an exceptional fleet—fascinating, I think, to many others as well. Of course, I missed altogether the big, prewar superliners, the *Rex* and the *Conte di Savoia*, but at New York I visited the classic *Saturnia* and *Vulcania* and the renovated *Conte Biancamano* and *Conte Grande*. They were the "old" Italian liners. With their rich woods, gilded carvings, marble and crystal, the thick draperies and carpets, the *Saturnia* and the *Vulcania* were just about the last-of-an-era when they sailed away on their final crossings out of New York in the spring of 1965. They were both a little frayed and certainly aged when I went aboard both of them in their final months with Italian Line.

But it was the postwar Italian Line ships that aroused and intrigued many of us. First, they were among the best-looking liners of their time—raked bows, single masts above the wheelhouse areas, and then one large smokestack. The evolution of design was quite apparent—the splendid *Giulio Cesare* and *Augustus* of 1951–52 clearly led to the superb *Andrea Doria* and *Cristoforo Colombo* of '53–54 and then to the magnificent *Leonardo Da Vinci* of 1960. It was perhaps those dominant, birdcage-like funnels on the *Michelangelo* and *Raffaello* (both of 1965) that made these ships quite different, perhaps a bit too radical. Nevertheless, they were always impressive to see. And we cannot forget some other Italian maritime masterpieces, away from the Italian Line itself, but mentioned herein, such as the modern-looking *Australia* class of seven sisters and near-sisters of Lloyd Triestino, the very handsome *Ausonia* of the Adriatica Line, and two more, the far larger Lloyd Triestino liners, the *Galileo Galilei* and the *Guglielmo Marconi*. And then there was Costa's very fine *Federico C.* and *Eugenio C.*

But it was the interiors that drew even more aficionados—devotees, if you will—to the Italian Line passenger fleet. No company had more modern, more contemporarily styled liners on the Atlantic in the 1950s and '60s. That prewar richness of heavy, polished woods and golden cherubs, the tiered crystal and the mixes of Delft tiles, Persian rugs and Moorish columns—the floating movie palace—were gone forever. The new 1950s decor was far simpler—illuminated, glass-top cocktail tables, chairs and sofas upholstered in velours, long strips of fluorescent lighting, and often reddish, always glossed linoleum floors. The woods tended to be blond or, at the very least, honey-colored. The lido decks remained much the same, however—tiled pools, cushioned deck chairs, and white tables supporting big multicolored umbrellas.

I associated the great Atlantic liners of yesteryear, particularly those in my youth, in the 1950s, with different elements. For the British Cunarders, it was fog. For the American passenger ships, it was sparkling care. For the Germans, it was midnight sailings. And for the Italian Line, it was summer. It was those vast lido decks, those colorful umbrellas, still very much the "Rivieras afloat." It was those mild-weather, mid-Atlantic crossings, the sunny Mediterranean destinations, the cheerful Italian songs. The sight of, say, the all-white, flag-bedecked *Leonardo Da Vinci* leaving New York harbor and bound for the likes of Lisbon and Cannes, Genoa and Naples, was pure magic.

Like Cunard and the French Line, the great Italian Line deserves to sail once again, in a photographic review. In all, the Company's history spanned forty-five years, from 1932 until 1977. When I came home from Europe in 1973, on the *Raffaello*, there were rumors of the end. The airlines had become unbeatable, the operational costs overwhelming. Another era was passing—a great play, as it were, was closing.

By coincidence, from a point along the Jersey shore, in 1975, I saw the *Raffaello* off on the horizon. In the poetic mists of an April afternoon, she was on her last outbound trip. It was ineffably sad. Soon, the regularity of sailings to the Mediterranean would be over. But now, in this book, in this collection of choice, mostly borrowed photographs, the great Italian liners reappear once again. Momentarily, it could almost be a summer's day at the Stazione Marittima in Genoa, and the *Conte di Savoia* or the *Cristoforo Colombo* is preparing to sail.

WILLIAM H. MILLER
Secaucus, New Jersey
Winter 1998

Picture Credits

Paolo Piccione Collection: pages 2, 3(top), 6, 7, 8(top), 9, 10, 11, 12, 13 (top), 15 (bottom), 17, 18, 21, 22, 23, 25, 27, 28, 29, 30, 31, 32(bottom), 33, 34, 36, 40, 41, 43(bottom), 44, 47, 50, 52(middle & bottom), 53, 54, 55, 56, 62(bottom), 63, 64, 67(bottom), 69, 70(bottom), 71, 72, 73, 77(top), 78, 79(bottom), 81, 86, 88, 89, 96, 97(bottom), 107(bottom), 109, 111, 113(bottom), 116(top), 119, 120, 121(top), 122(bottom), 123, 124, 125(middle & bottom), 126, 127(bottom)

Cronican Arroyo Collection, pages 4, 5, 8 (bottom), 13 (bottom), 19 (bottom), 32 (top), 37, 43(top), 45. 46, 49, 58(top), 59(bottom), 61, 62(top), 65, 66, 67 (top), 68, 75, 76, 77(bottom), 84, 85, 91, 93, 94, 95, 99, 100(top), 104, 105, 106(top), 107(top), 108

Richard Faber Collection, pages 3(bottom), 15(top), 16, 24, 48, 51, 52(top), 57, 58(bottom), 101, 102, 103

Sal Scannella Collection, pages 79(top & middle), 80, 100(bottom), 110(top), 116(bottom)

Tom Greene Collection, pages 38, 39, 42, 114-115, 121(bottom)

Maurizio Elisio Collection, pages 70(top), 106(bottom), 127(top)

Antonio Scrimali, pages 82, 117

Italian Line, pages 112, 122(top), 125(top)

Roger Sherlock, page 87; Flying Camera, Inc., page 90(top); Alex Duncan, page 90(bottom); Newport News Shipbuilding & Dry Dock Company, page 92; Costa Line, page 97(top); Roger Scozzofazzo, page 110(bottom); Ernest Arroyo Collection, page 101; Moran Towing & Transportation Company, page 113(top); James Ciani, page 128(top); Gregory Vossos, 197; Costa Cruises, page 129; Carnival Cruise Lines, page 130; Author collection, page 19(top)

Introduction

To introduce a new book on Italian ocean liners by Bill Miller is like being asked to baptize a newborn baby.

A book of this kind is essentially a creature of love: the author has an intimate knowledge of all the splendid liners built and operated by the Italian Line from 1932 until 1977. It was a glorious period for crossing the Atlantic with style, and Bill Miller loved all the great ships. During his varied travels, he has met many of the ships' masters and senior officers and executives, who gave him an intimate picture of a great company with long tradition and pride in service. For me personally, this book is a nostalgic voyage back to the time when first-class passengers represented the real aristocracy in finance, diplomacy, arts and in the the professional world.

As a young officer, out of the Genoa Merchant Marine Academy, I lived in a dream world on board sleek, elegant white ships bearing names of Italian Renaissance geniuses and Roman emperors. Voyage after voyage, I felt the sheer energy of all the passengers coming from the far corners of the world, speaking dozens of languages, rich and poor, old and young, men and women, an amazing collection of humanity, all strangers sharing the fantastic experience of crossing the Atlantic together.

I remember the first time that the captain invited me, a junior cadet, for dinner at his table and later to the grand ballroom. It was kind of an invitation for young officers to the strict etiquette of the ship and to the learning process of discipline and responsibility. In those days, it was *de rigueur* in first class for gentlemen to wear tuxedoes while ladies displayed a different gala dress every night. Although we were supposed to dance only with the unattached, mature ladies, we had the freedom to look around and indulge in those eye contacts more explicit than a thousand words. On one of those gala nights, sailing between Barcelona and Rio de Janeiro aboard the *Augustus*, I met a young Chilean girl returning home from a European tour. After a brief romance, I knew my career as a seagoing "Latin lover" was over.

While I often reminisce about the many celebrities I met during my ten years at sea, in my personal experience it was tourist class that offered a genuine sample of humanity and a wealth of characters. Each crossing had its own story for many passengers. For the emigrants leaving their beautiful ancient villages in southern Italy to start a new life in the "New World," it was an epic voyage to the unknown. America, both North and South, had a powerful attraction for young people from Europe for a good part of this century. And until the 1960s the "boat" was the only way to go.

As a young purser in tourist class, I met thousands of these simple, solid men and women. I could see the anxiety and sadness in the eyes of the poor emigrants, but most of all their determination and hope. For many of them the trip from Genoa, Naples, Trieste, or Palermo to New York, Buenos Aires, Santos, or La Guaira was the first time out of their Italian hometown; for all, it was the event of their life. Those few days spent on board an Italian ship was the last bit of their country, where both crew and passengers ate the same food and understood their language, their pain, and their drama.

Upon arriving at the first American port, there was the sudden impact with the new reality: the long immigration process, the searches through their ragged baggage in the terminal, the customs inspection, and finally the emotional embrace with relatives or friends waiting for them behind the wooden fences. The United States, often the country of their dream, was now a reality.

And then there was the crew.

Italian Line passenger ships were special not only for their elegant design and decor, their technology, and their art collections, but also for their impeccable service. From the captain down, everybody had to go through strict training and annual evaluation; the best people were normally assigned to the newest and most prestigious ships. All officers were licensed from the rigorous merchant marine schools in Italy, and many had attended the Naval Academy at Leghorn.

The staff in the hotel department was carefully selected and trained as well, usually at the hotel schools in northern Italy, Switzerland, or France. Waiters knew the ingredients and preparation of each dish served in the first and cabin class, and could speak two or three languages. Their service was a show of perfection and virtuosity. Watching them boning a sole or peeling an orange was such a delight! The cooks, 72 in all on the larger ships, were guided by a gifted master chef, who had both enormous prestige and authority. Every gala dinner was a triumph of good taste and culinary prowess.

Unfortunately, these traditions became the victim of political as well as social events during the late 1960s. A combination of factors contributed to the demise of the Italian Line. Management did not have the foresight to understand that liner service across the Atlantic was doomed by the airplane and instead continued to build large, powerful ships to challenge the airlines. They completely disregarded operational costs.

Unions became stronger, inflexible, and more influential; wildcat strikes were declared by young, arrogant ship delegates for the most inane reasons and against the advice of their very own national leaders. Some crew members, politically indoctrinated, had the misguided certainty that the Government would never dare close down a national institution like the Italian Line and would keep subsidizing their demands forever. Top management, paralyzed by endless negotiations between Government agencies and unions, had neither the vision nor the energy to stop the increasing losses. The shocking oil price increases of 1973 struck the final blow.

The end came swiftly and forcefully. In 1975, the Government decided by a large majority to close the Italian Line passenger services. Most of the ships were soon laid-up. The *Michelangelo* and the *Raffaello*, the pride of Italy, were sold to the Shah of Iran, to be used as floating quarters for the Iranian Navy. Over a century of tradition and prestige were suddenly gone. It was a bitter lesson that, unfortunately, too many subsidized companies around the world have not yet learned.

In this book, Bill Miller reviews the *belle epoque* of Italian transatlantic vessels with the eyes of a historian who wants very much to educate and enlighten his readers on the joy and romance of ocean travel by a classic liner. All of us who lived through those marvelous days on those magnificent ships, either as passengers, immigrants, officers, or crew members, are indebted to Bill for bringing back to life the splendor and the magic of the Italian Line ships.

Nicola Arena
New York City,
December 1997

Nicola Arena is currently president of Mediterranean Shipping Company (USA) Inc., Italian owned and one of the world's most important operators of cargo vessels as well as several cruise ships.

~1~
The Early Fleet

"Italia,"—Italia Flotta Riunite Cosulich–Lloyd Sabaudo–NGI—the Italian Line to North Americans—came into being on January 2, 1932. The Lloyd Sabaudo and the Navigazione Generale Italiana, with the coordination of the Cosulich Line, were joined in the same financial group. While the new Italian Line was based at Genoa, Cosulich still maintained a separate management at Trieste. But in effect, Italy's three mightiest Atlantic shipping lines were now one.

There were two important reasons for the formation of the new company. The first was, of course, the serious effects of the Depression. Italian passenger ships were experiencing a tremendous drop in passenger traffic, and so all wasteful competition had to be eliminated. The second reason, possibly more important, was simply for prestige. Premier Benito Mussolini's government wanted Italy to have a stronger position in transatlantic passenger shipping. More specifically, Mussolini wanted Italy to be equal to the British, the French, and the Germans. The government had already encouraged the NGI to build the 51,000-ton superliner *Rex* and the Lloyd Sabaudo to build the 48,500-ton *Conte di Savoia*. It seemed foolish to have these two Italian luxury liners as competitors after they began service in the summer and fall of 1932. Instead, so Mussolini himself felt, they should be running mates, jointly carrying the Italian colors in triumph and success. Actually, the three companies had had a pooling agreement since 1928, but these two new superliners made it desirable to consolidate even further.

The Italian Line started with a registered capital of 720,000,000 lira and a fleet of twenty-two ships totaling 400,500 tons. NGI had the 32,000-ton sister ships *Augustus* and *Roma* on the New York run and the near-sisters *Duilio* and *Giulio Cesare* sailing to the east coast of South America. Lloyd Sabaudo had their *Conte Grande* and *Conte Biancamano* on the New York run and the *Conte Rosso* and *Conte Verde* to South America. Finally, Cosulich had the *Saturnia* and *Vulcania* in New York service and were planning a pair of ships, *Neptunia* and *Oceania*, for South American sailings. Clearly, there was duplication.

The *Augustus* left Genoa on December 28, 1931, five days before the actual amalgamation took place, and reached New York on January 9th. When she sailed two days later, on the 11th, on a West Indies cruise, her funnels had been repainted in the new Italian Line colors (red, green, and white) and flew the new company's flag. The latter combined the emblems of Italy's two leading ports, Genoa and Trieste. More specifically, the design carried the cross of St. George (red on a white field) and the white halyard of Trieste on a red field. The actual distinction of the first transatlantic sailing under the new Italian Line fell to the *Conte Biancamano*. She left Genoa on January 8th, bound for New York via Villefranche, Naples, and Gibraltar, in the new company colors.

By 1933, the Italian Line had a worldwide passenger fleet. The *Rex*, the *Conte di Savoia*, the *Augustus*, and the *Roma* sailed in the Genoa–New York express service. The *Conte Biancamano*, the *Conte Grande* and later the *Augustus* sailed to South America—Rio de Janeiro, Santos, Montevideo, and Buenos Aires from Genoa. The *Duilio* and the *Giulio Cesare* inaugurated a new service from Genoa, Marseilles, and Gibraltar to Dakar, Capetown, and Durban. The *Saturnia* and the *Vulcania* sailed the North Atlantic to New York, but out of the Adriatic, from Trieste and Venice. The *Neptunia* and the *Oceania* also went on the South American route. Finally, the *Conte Rosso* and the *Conte Verde* were used on the long-haul Genoa–Shanghai run. They were, however, soon transferred to another Italian shipowner, Lloyd Triestino.

Conte Rosso and Conte Verde

Launched at Glasgow in December 1917, an earlier *Conte Rosso* was immediately commandeered by the British and completed as the aircraft carrier HMS *Argus*. She became a training ship by 1937, and survived the Second World War, only to be sent to the shipbreakers in 1946. Lloyd Sabaudo had launched a new *Conte Rosso* in the winter of 1921 and saw it completed a year later; the *Conte Verde* (*above*), shown in February 1929 as she passed the *Conte Grande* in mid-ocean, was launched in October 1921 and completed in April 1923. Two splendid ships, they were among Italy's largest liners for a time. Used on both the Genoa–New York and Genoa–Rio–Buenos Aires routes, they were integrated into the newly formed Italian Line in January 1932. Soon afterward, in the following summer, they were transferred to the Far Eastern run, from Genoa to Shanghai via Suez. The exact routing was from Trieste, Venice, Genoa, and Naples via Port Said to Bombay, Colombo, Singapore, Manila, and Shanghai. [Built by William Beardmore & Company Limited, Glasgow, Scotland, 1923. 18,765 gross tons; 559 feet long; 74 feet wide. Steam turbines, twin screw. Service speed 18½ knots. 2,400 passengers (230 first class, 290 second class, 1,880 third class).]

The ballroom aboard *Conte Rosso* (*opposite, top*) was a rich neo-classical creation. The highlight in ways was the large Beaux Arts chandelier. A piano at the far end in this photo sometimes was replaced by a large, quite distinctive chair in which the captain sat during recitals and special presentations and performances.

The winter garden, as seen here (*opposite, bottom*) aboard the *Conte Verde*, was a standard ingredient in the design of most transatlantic passenger liners. It was a quiet space, of course, a refuge—with its rattan furniture and plants and therefore garden-like effect—on less comfortable days at sea.

The Early Fleet 3

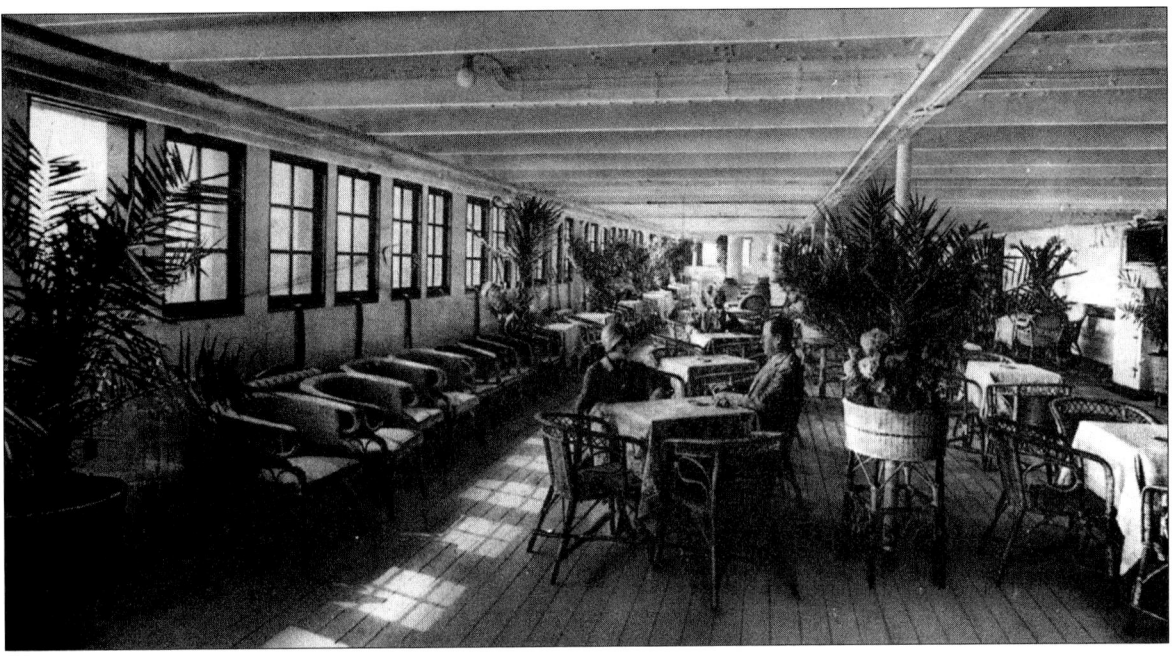

Shortly after their transfer to the Genoa–Shanghai run in the summer of 1932, both the *Conte Rosso* and *Conte Verde (above)* were transferred to another Italian shipping line, Lloyd Triestino, who had important interests in the Middle and Far Eastern trades. The ships' accommodations were greatly reduced to suit this trade. Aboard the *Conte Verde*, for example, the berthing was rearranged as 250 in first class, 170 in second class, and 220 in third class. In September 1936, the *Conte Verde* was nearly lost when she grounded on Cape Collinson off Hong Kong during a hurricane. She was freed only with great difficulty. Unfortunately, both ships had tragic wartime endings.

The *Conte Rosso* became an Italian troopship in 1940. A year later, on May 24, 1941, she was sunk while carrying 2,500 soldiers in an otherwise heavily protected convoy bound for Tripoli. Two torpedoes were fired on her by a British submarine, and she sank 15 miles east of Syracuse on Sicily. There were well over 800 casualties. Early in the war the *Conte Verde* was interned at Shanghai. In 1942, she was chartered to the Japanese for several prisoner-of-war exchange voyages between Japan and China. In 1943, just after the Italian capitulation, her Italian crew deliberately sank the ship to avoid capture, especially by the Japanese. Soon afterward, the Japanese government had the ship salvaged, towed to Japan, and refitted as a troopship. But her days were numbered. In 1944, she was sunk during an American air raid on Maizuru. She was salvaged in June 1949, only to be sold to Mitsui & Company for scrapping in 1951.

4   *The Early Fleet*

Duilio and *Giulio Cesare* (1922)

These were the largest ships in the NGI, the Navigazione Generale Italiana, and were acclaimed as Italy's finest liners to date. The *Duilio* was actually laid down in 1914, launched in January 1916, then had her construction halted owing to the First World War. Work resumed in 1920, and she left Genoa on her maiden voyage to New York on October 30, 1923. The *Giulio Cesare* arrived a year and one-half earlier—having a maiden voyage from Genoa to Rio de Janeiro and Buenos Aires in May 1922, followed by one to New York that August. The *Duilio* (***below***) is shown sailing from New York's Pier 97, at West 57th Street, on November 20, 1923. [Built by Ansaldo Shipyards, Genoa, Italy, 1923. 24,281 gross tons; 635 feet long; 76 feet wide. Steam turbines, quadruple screw. Service speed 19 knots. 1,550 passengers (280 first class, 670 second class, 600 third class).]

In January 1932, the *Duilio* (*above*), shown passing the *Conte di Savoia* in October 1933, and the *Giulio Cesare* were transferred to the Italian Line. Soon afterward, they began passenger service to South Africa from Italy. Their passenger accommodations were soon modified as well, dropping to 170 in first class, 170 in second class, and 300 in tourist class.

Interior spaces on these two ships were luxurious, especially in first class. Aboard the *Duilio* the gallery (*opposite, top*) and the smoking room (*opposite, bottom*) were particularly impressive. They attracted travelers of wealth, power, and nobility. Elena of Orleans, the Grand Duchess of Aosta (standing in the right foreground), is seen during a ceremony in the ballroom of the *Duilio* (*left*) on an African sailing in May 1939.

6   *The Early Fleet*

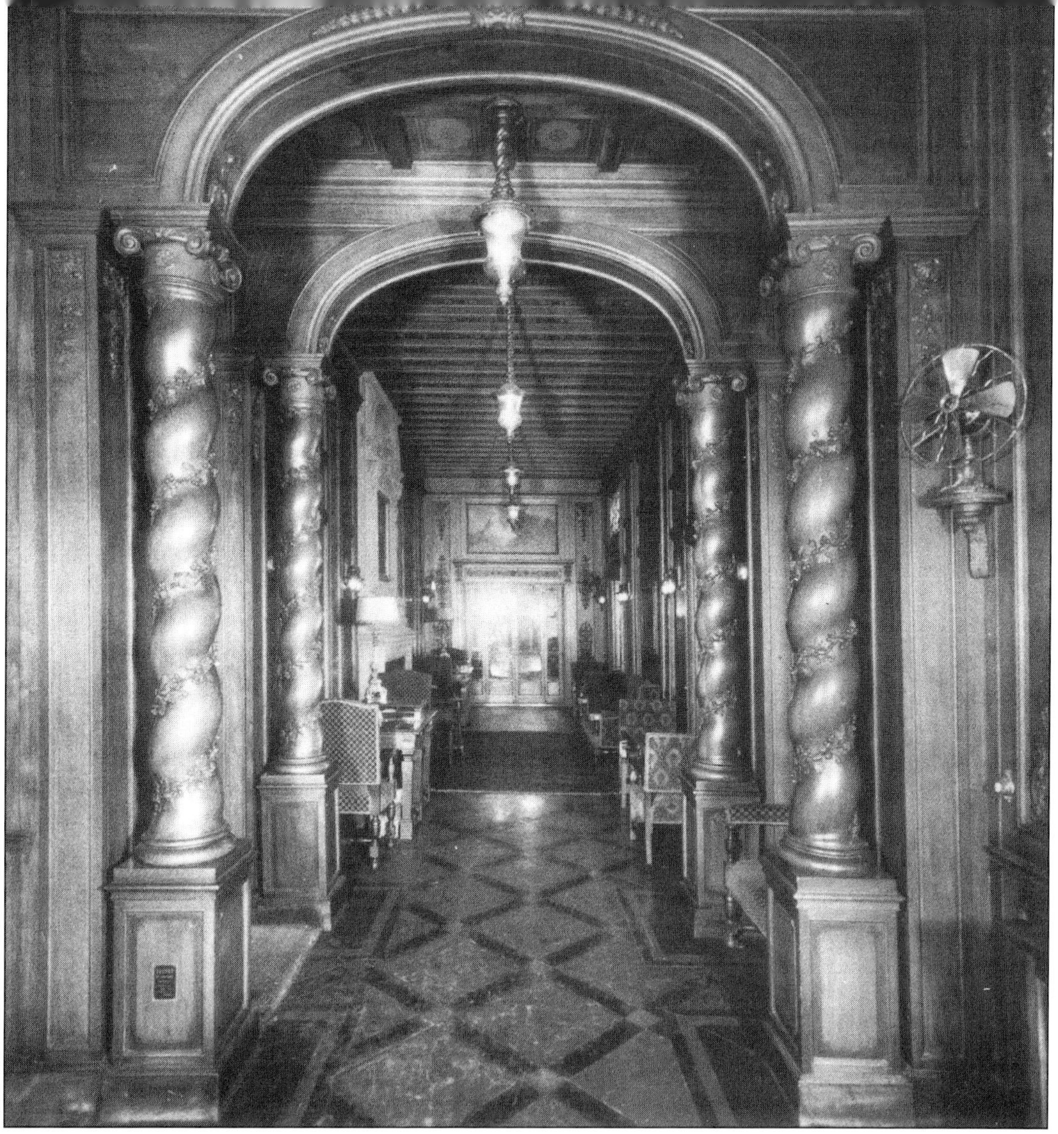

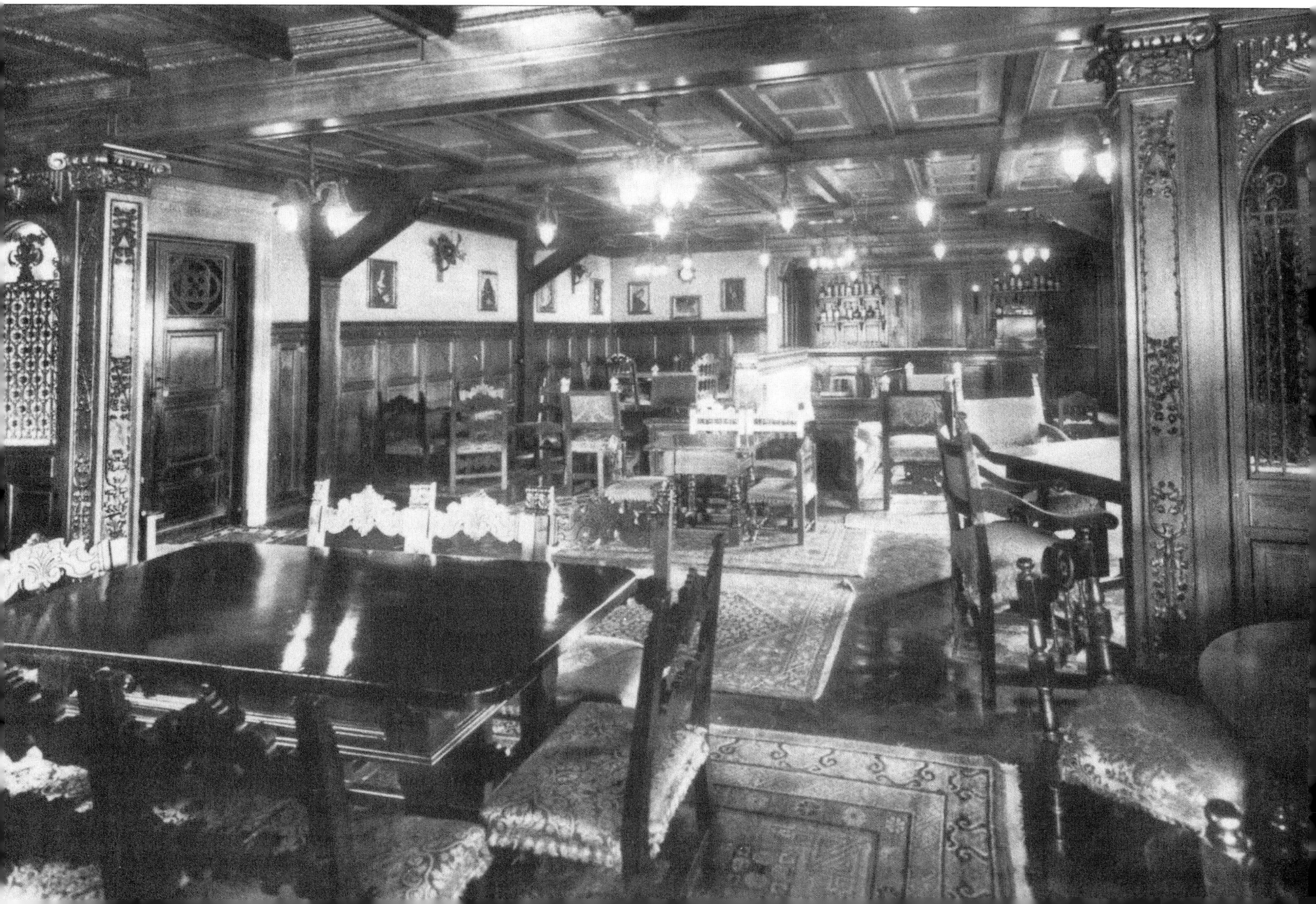

Four Italian Line passenger ships *(above)* were photographed together at Genoa in 1933: From left to right, the *Rex*, the *Giulio Cesare*, the *Roma*, and the *Duilio*.

As they continued their South African sailings, both the *Duilio* and the *Giulio Cesare* were transferred to Lloyd Triestino in 1937. In 1940, after Italy went to war, both ships were laid up. Both would become war losses. In 1942, they were chartered to the International Red Cross for use as hospital, evacuation, and exchange ships. Mostly, they were used between Italy and East Africa. The *Duilio* was, however, sunk during an Allied air raid on Trieste on July 10, 1944. Her remains were salvaged in 1948 and sold to local scrappers. The *Giulio Cesare* *(below)*, with the *Rex* in the left background, capsized after being hit during another Allied raid on Trieste, September 11, 1944. Supposedly, she was sunk by the U.S. Air Force when the Nazis were caught using her as a troop transport in Red Cross colors. Her remains were broken up in 1948 as well.

Conte Biancamano

Two of the grandest, most ornate, and most popular Italian liners of the years between the wars were the near-sisters *Conte Biancamano* and *Conte Grande*. They followed the earlier *Conte Rosso* and *Conte Verde* in the Lloyd Sabaudo fleet. The *Conte Biancamano* (**below**), launched in April 1925, entered the Genoa–New York trade that November. [Built by William Beardmore & Company Limited, Glasgow, Scotland, 1925. 24,416 gross tons; 653 feet long; 76 feet wide. Steam turbines, twin screw. Service speed 20 knots. 1,750 passengers (280 first class, 420 second class, 390 third class, 660 fourth class).]

The first-class ballroom aboard the *Conte Biancamano* (**left**) was an equally splendid space—three decks high and with a fireplace at the far end and a domed center section. Regrettably, like all the grand rooms aboard the *Conte Grande*, it would be gutted and removed during the early years of the Second World War, when the Americans converted most liners they seized into troop transports.

The Early Fleet 9

Conte Grande

This ship differed slightly from her earlier near-sister in that she was Italian-built. Shown (*above*) in 1933 during a cruise call at Palma de Majorca, she was, like the *Conte Biancamano*, transferred to the Italian Line in January 1932. Used in the New York trade as well as to South America, she also went cruising in the 1930s. Her thirty-two day Mediterranean cruise from New York in January 1933 called at Madeira, Gibraltar, Palma, Cannes, Genoa, Naples, Piraeus, Rhodes, Haifa, Alexandria, Naples, Cannes, and Gibraltar. Minimum inside rooms in first class were priced from $510, minimum tourist class rooms from $225. A suite—with bedroom, sitting room, and full bath—was priced at $1,200 per person. The half-day tour at Cannes cost $2, the all-day coach tour at Naples $3.50, and the five-day overland visit from Haifa to Jerusalem, Cairo, and Alexandria was set at $95. A deck chair could be hired for the entire cruise at $2 and a blanket for an additional $2. [Built by Stabilimento Tecnico Shipyard, Trieste, Italy, 1927. 25,661 gross tons; 652 feet long; 78 feet wide. Steam turbines, twin screws. Service speed 19 knots. 1,718 passengers (578 first class, 420 second class, 720 third class).]

The grand smoking room aboard the *Conte Grande* (**left**) had a rich, clublike ambiance. It included a great fireplace as well as a convenient bar off to the side. It also had a tremendous sense of drama about it. The design of this room was quite eclectic, with Delft tiles and French gargoyles and with Persian carpets covering the parquet floors. The ballroom (**below**) had a magnificent gallery, an oval dance floor, and an aviary. One of the most lavish shipboard rooms of the 1920s, its design was broadly based on the style of the Mogul period in India. The arches in this three-deck-high space suggest something out of the *Arabian Nights* and, closer to home, the grand American movie theatres built during this prosperous period.

With its cool tile floors, rattan chairs, and touches of greenery, the veranda aboard the *Conte Grande* (***above***) was often a refuge from steamy afternoons in the Mediterranean or the rough seas of a wintertime Atlantic passage. A grand stairway descended into the first-class restaurant (***below***). Said to be decorated in the "grand manner" by Italian Line, it is clearly very ornate and typically "Italian, rich and gilded." The company's promotional material said of this space, "The lofty dining room . . . where every meal is an event of rare delight . . . under soft lights . . . and amid decorations of colorful artistry and brilliance."

The indoor pool *(left)* aboard the *Conte Grande*—advertised in the early 1930s by the Italian Line as the "largest of its kind afloat"—was quite extraordinary. Unlike the usual athletic facility, it was decorated in Japanese style, with murals, a little bridge over the pool, and the colors and smaller details of old Japan. Adjacent was a fully equipped gym, steam room, showers, and changing rooms.

Fortunately, both the *Conte Biancamano* and the *Conte Grande* survived the Second World War. The *Conte Biancamano* was seized by the Americans in the Panama Canal Zone on March 30, 1941, and taken over by U.S. Naval units. Shown *(below)* alongside is the USS *Mallard*, from which the American boarding party went on the liner. She was one of twenty-eight Italian ships seized by the U.S. forces in their territorial waters. The 500 crew members from the Italian liner were later transferred to New York. The *Conte Grande*, which was laid up at Santos in 1940, was officially seized by the Brazilian government at that port on August 22, 1941. In the following April, she was transferred to the United States government, taken to an American shipyard, and rebuilt as a troopship. In August 1942, the former *Conte Biancamano* began sailing as the USS *Hermitage*, and a month later the ex-*Conte Grande* entered service as the USS *Monticello*. Both ships would later be decommissioned and finally returned to the Italians in 1947.

~2~
Castles at Sea

Following the destruction and disarray of the First World War, the transatlantic ocean liner business was, in some ways, slow to rebuild and regenerate. A sense of caution, of moderation, prevailed in steamship company boardrooms in London and Liverpool, in Bremen, Hamburg, and Paris, and at Genoa. Construction materials were often in short supply, shipyards were overbooked, and reconstruction budgets often tight. Furthermore, and perhaps most importantly, the once lucrative third-class/steerage trade was greatly reduced by the U.S. government's new immigration quotas of 1921. The flow of 1.2 million migrants that had crossed westbound in, say, 1907 was suddenly reduced to a scant 150,000 by 1924. The quick profits made by prewar ships were suddenly cut as new, improved tourist-class quarters were often fitted in those lower-deck spaces. Times had changed.

The British still had the "largest" and "fastest" liners afloat with the likes of the *Majestic* and the *Mauretania*, but they were of prewar build. New construction mostly meant very conservative 15–20,000 tonners. Somewhat more enthusiastic and optimistic, however, the French added the 34,500-ton *Paris* in 1921 and the 43,100-ton *Ile de France* in 1927. Although still restricted by their Allied victors, the Germans managed to add one big liner, the 32,500-ton, 1,725-passenger *Columbus* in 1924. The Italians, rather slow in taking a permanent place in the Atlantic liner business, started in the early twenties with sets of sisters and near-sisters—the *Conte Rosso* and *Conte Verde* in 1921–23, the *Giulio Cesare* and *Duilio* in 1922–23, the *Conte Biancamano* in 1925, and the *Conte Grande* in 1927. But their two biggest, fastest, and perhaps grandest entries of the twenties were the 32,600-ton sister ships *Roma* and *Augustus*.

"The *Roma* and *Augustus* were ornate, richly decorated ships," said passenger ship historian Everett Viez. "They were like floating palaces, like castles. They were so rich in their gilded Baroque stylings that they made a lasting impression on everyone who saw them. They were the ultimate Italian liners in the late twenties." Built by the Ansaldo shipyard at Sestri Ponente, near Genoa, they were commissioned over a year apart—the *Roma* in September 1926, the *Augustus* in November 1927. In her 711-foot-long hull, the *Augustus* carried as many as 2,210 passengers. The ship was divided into 302 berths in opulent first class, 504 in less-fancy second class, and 1,404 in austere third class.

Owned by the NGI, Navigazione Generale Italiana, the two big ships were later integrated—at Premier Mussolini's instigation—into the neatly formed, combined Italian Line of 1932. In their early years, they ran the Italian "express service"—from Naples, Genoa, Villefranche, and Gibraltar to New York. Later repainted with white hulls, they were used on the Italy-South America run, to Rio de Janeiro, Santos, Montevideo, and Buenos Aires. They also sailed on cruises such as six-week jaunts out of New York to ports around the entire Mediterranean.

The 51,000-ton *Rex* and the 48,500-ton *Conte di Savoia* became Italy's premier luxury liners in 1932. Glorious ships in every way, but a third ship—either the *Augustus* or the *Roma*—was needed to maintain a weekly express run on the North Atlantic. There were rumors in 1938–39 that a third superliner would be built to join the *Rex* and *Conte di Savoia*. Some rumors even suggested a three-stacker as large as 60,000 tons. "The government and therefore the Italian Line changed their minds," noted Maurizio Eliseo, an authority on Italian passenger ships. "The revised plan was to rebuild the *Augustus* and the *Roma*. The plans called for a greatly altered exterior—one funnel and one mast placed above the wheelhouse area—that looked like the *Giulio Cesare* and the *Augustus* of 1951–52. They wanted to change the original steam turbines and diesels [from 1926–27] to Fiat diesels to increase their service speeds. Fiat planned to build eight diesels, but only five were actually made. They were kept in storage during the Second World War. Afterward, in the late 1940s, two went to the new *Giulio Cesare*, two to the new *Augustus*, and one to a postwar Italian Line freighter."

Plans changed once again for the *Roma* and *Augustus* when, during the war, Mussolini's navy had them redesigned and then rebuilt as large aircraft carriers. They were in fact the largest passenger ships ever so converted. Later seized by the Nazis, they were finally victims of Allied bombings. When the war ended, in the spring of 1945, both ships were lying in Genoa harbor—sunk, gutted, beyond repair. They finished their days at the scrapyard.

"In the 1990s, long after the ship had left commercial service, the statue of the Goddess Roma that was aboard the *Roma* was found behind a staircase in a small Genoa shop," added Maurizio Eliseo. "Created by Angelo Zanelli, it is nine feet tall and made of Carrara marble. It was put up for sale and priced at $10,000."

Roma

The *Roma* was launched on February 26, 1926, at the Ansaldo yard. She left Genoa on her maiden crossing to New York on September 21st. The *Augustus* followed (***above***), in her original Navigazione Generale Italiana stack colors, being launched also at the Ansaldo yard on December 13, 1926. Her maiden voyage was to the east coast of South America from Genoa, departing on November 10, 1927. A maiden sailing to New York followed in August 1928. [Built by Ansaldo Shipyards, Genoa, Italy, 1926. 32,583 gross tons; 709 feet long; 82 feet wide. Steam turbines, quadruple screw. Service speed 22 knots. 1,675 passengers (375 first class, 600 second class, 700 third class).]

The *Roma*'s first-class dining salon (***below***) was also styled after an 18th-century palazzo. It had two levels, both on separate decks, and was capped by a great domed center section. Along the sides were tall windows overlooking the sea. Aboard the *Augustus* there was also a Japanese grillroom for smaller, private dinner parties.

Augustus (1928)

The *Roma* and the *Augustus* (***above***), seen from her passing sister ship, were transferred over to the Italian Line in January 1932. Thereafter, both ships sailed on the express run to New York, to the east coast of South America, and on cruises. Until the advent of the *Rex* and the *Conte di Savoia* in 1932, they were the largest Italian liners as well as the largest ships based anywhere in the Mediterranean. [Built by Ansaldo Shipyards, Genoa, Italy, 1928. 32,650 gross tons; 711 feet long; 82 feet wide. M.A.N. diesels, quadruple screw. Service speed 19 knots. 2,210 passengers (302 first class, 504 second class, 1,404 third class).]

The first-class ballroom aboard the *Roma* (***opposite***) was patterned in the beautiful Baroque of an 18th-century Italian palazzo. Italian Line said of it, "The perfect room for brilliant soirees."

16 Castles at Sea

Castles at Sea 17

The *Augustus* (***above***), shown at Naples, and the *Roma* were very popular cruise ships in the 1930s. They ran short cruises, such as New York to the Caribbean and, in summer, up to the Canadian Maritimes, but occasionally offered long, luxurious sailings as well. On January 4, 1933, for example, the *Augustus* left New York on a 129-day around-the-world cruise. It called at Funchal, Gibraltar, Cannes, Monte Carlo, Genoa, Naples, Tripoli, Phaleron (for Athens), Haifa, Port Suez, Bombay, Colombo, Penang, Belawan Deli, Singapore, Paknam (for Bangkok), Tandjong-Priok (Batavia), Samarang, Pandang Bay (Bali), Zamboanga, Manila, Hong Kong, Shanghai, Chinwangtao (China), Miyajima, Kobe, Yokohama, Honolulu, Hilo, San Francisco, Los Angeles, Balboa, Cristobal, and finally Havana before returning to New York. Minimum fare was $2,100. Shore excursions included a four-day overland tour in Palestine at $25, a ten-day overland in India and Ceylon for $300, a visit to the Great Wall in China for $10, and a three-day overland in California from San Francisco to Los Angeles at $48.50. The *Augustus* is seen here in home waters, at Naples.

Fateful gathering (***opposite, top***): On the eve of the Nazi attack on Poland on August 31, 1939, six passenger ships gather along New York's Luxury Liner Row. The peaceful, luxury days are just about over for most of them. From top to bottom are the *Bremen*, North German Lloyd; the *Normandie*, French Line; the *Aquitania*, Cunard Line; the *Roma*, Italian Line; the *Southern Prince*; and the *Monarch of Bermuda*, both Furness Lines.

While there were rather lavish plans to rebuild both the *Roma* and the *Augustus* in 1939–40, these never came about owing to the outbreak of War. Both were laid up for a time and then taken over by the Italian navy, to be rebuilt as aircraft carriers. New, high-speed, 30-knot turbines went into the *Roma* as her rebuilding commenced. By 1943, renamed *Aquila*, she was just about complete when she fell into Nazi hands. She was never put to any use. On June 20, 1944, she was heavily damaged during the Allied air raids on Genoa. A year or so later, on April 19th, she was deliberately sunk by the Italians so as to prevent the retreating Nazi forces from sinking her themselves in an attempt to block the harbor entrance at Genoa. Beyond any form of repair, she was salvaged in 1946 and the wrecked hull towed to La Spezia (***opposite, bottom***), where it remained for five years. It was finally broken up in 1951. A similar fate befell the *Augustus*. She too was converted to an aircraft carrier, with the name *Falco* finally giving way to *Sparviero*. She too fell into Nazi hands after the Italian capitulation in September 1944. Weeks later, on the 25th of that same month, the Nazi high command ordered her sunk to block the entry to Genoa harbor. After the war, she too was salvaged in 1946, and her remains were sold to the breakers. Her last pieces were hauled ashore in 1947.

18 Castles at Sea

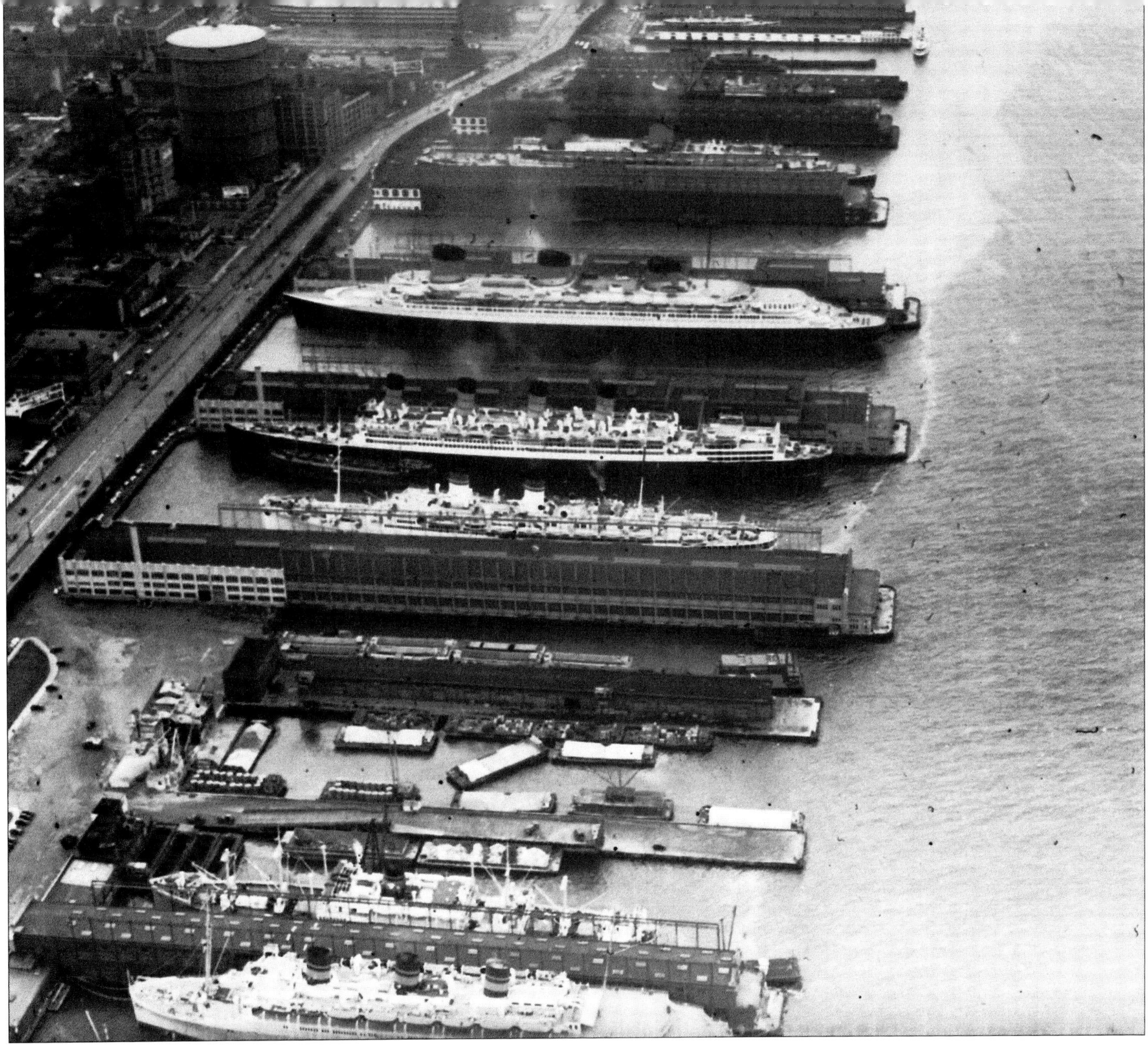

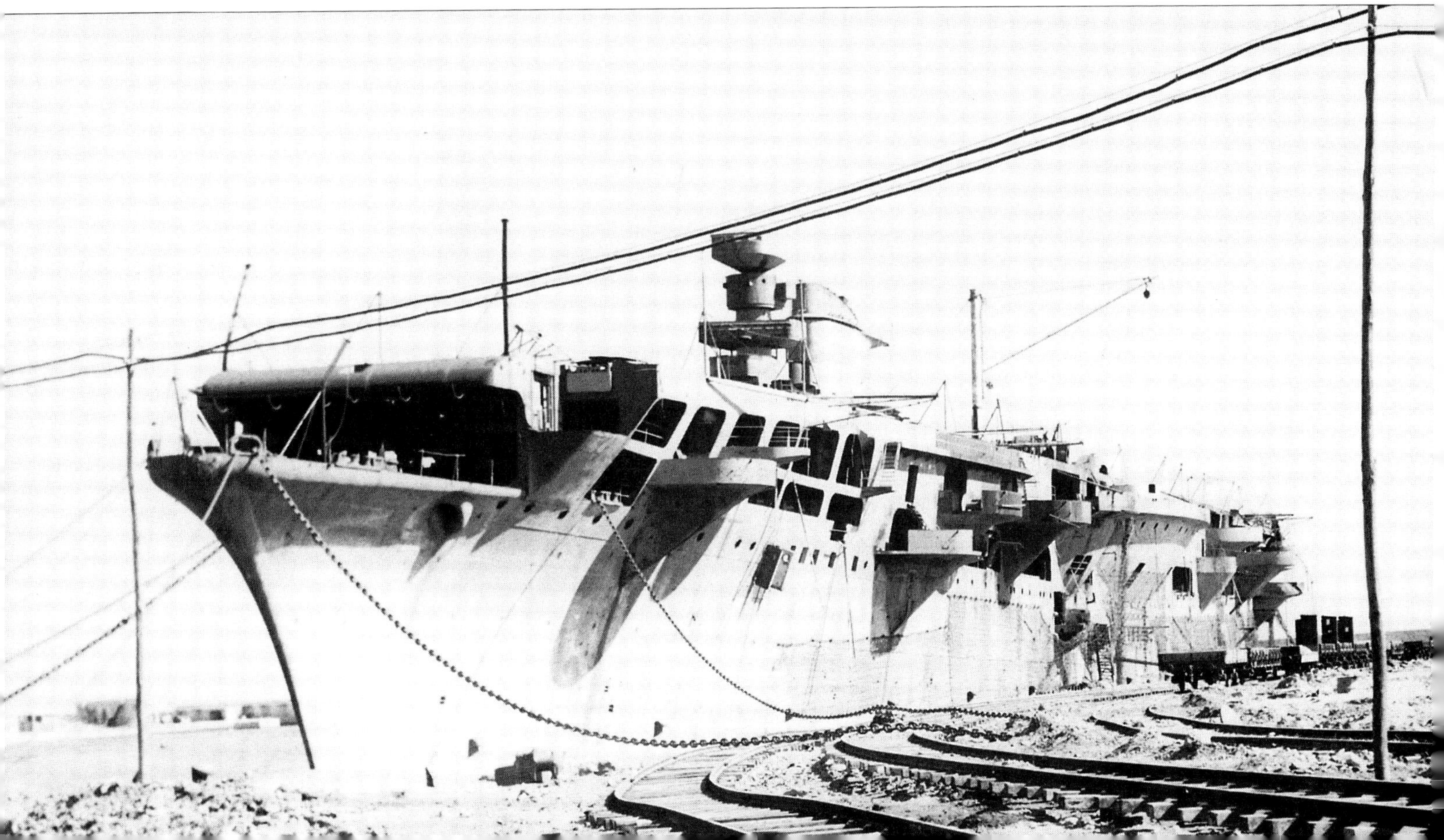

~3~
Classic Motor Liners

The brothers Callisto and Alberto Cosulich had formed the Unione Austriaca di Navigazione in 1903, then reestablished it, in 1919, under Italian instead of Austrian management. In that post-World-War-I era, the company was renamed Cosulich Societa Triestina di Navigazione—the Cosulich Line.

Cosulich's primary passenger ships by the mid-twenties were the 12,567-ton *Presidente Wilson*, which had been their *Kaiser Franz Josef I* before the war, and the 8,145-ton *Martha Washington*. Together, these ships ran a regular Atlantic service between Trieste, Patras, Palermo, Naples, Algiers, and Lisbon and New York. At the same time, the seven Italian-flag passenger lines on the North Atlantic had been reduced to four, with the three most important being Navigazione Generale Italiana, Lloyd Sabaudo, and Cosulich. The first two had added new passenger ships of approximately 20,000 tons. In addition, NGI was already planning the 32,000-ton sisters *Roma* and *Augustus*, and Sabaudo had orders for 25,000-ton near-sisters, *Conte Biancamano* and *Conte Grande*. Certainly, Cosulich had to have new, improved tonnage as well. And so the 24,000-ton motor liners *Saturnia* and *Vulcania* came into being.

The mid- and late-twenties were a time of maritime innovation and the beginning of the modern era for passenger ship design. The 18,000-ton Swedish liner *Gripsholm* had been the North Atlantic's first major diesel-driven liner when she was introduced in November 1925. After she proved herself in Atlantic service, more and more motor liners were built. The big, 32,600-ton *Augustus* arrived in the fall of 1927. Although her sister ship *Roma* had the traditional steam turbine propulsion, NGI put M.A.N.-type diesels in the *Augustus*. The latter was soon dubbed the "world's largest motor ship of any kind."

Diesels created a new external style—long, low profiles capped by a squattish stack or stacks. The three-funnel, traditional-looking *Ile de France* arrived in May 1927, the three-stack Dutch *Statendam* in April 1929, and even more notably, the *Queen Mary*, seven years later. These new "stump stack," motor liners presented a whole new look—appreciated by some, derided by others.

In early 1928, the Dutch added the 15,600-ton *Christiaan Huygens*, with its single, smallish stack shaped like a paint can. Union Castle Line's *Llangibby Castle* and *Dunbar Castle* of 1929 each sported two squat stacks. Their design led to larger versions, including a trio of sisters—the *Carnarvon Castle*, the *Winchester Castle*, and the *Warwick Castle*. Another British company, Royal Mail Lines, added two mighty motor liners of its own, the *Asturias* and the *Alcantara*. Then there was a pair of large liners for the White Star Line, the lean-looking *Britannic* of 1930 and the *Georgic* of 1932.

Cosulich's *Saturnia* and *Vulcania* were splendid ships in every way. They were introduced in February and December 1928, then joined the Italian Line schedules beginning in January 1932. (Cosulich was, however, not fully amalgamated into the Italian Line until 1937.)

"They were two of the most charming liners ever to sail the Atlantic," said Everett Viez. "At first, we discounted them because of their stump, flat stacks. But on the inside, they were Italian Baroque to the hilt. They were cathedrals gone to sea! Historically, they introduced the private veranda. Today, it is very popular as the private terrace or balcony. But on the *Saturnia* and the *Vulcania*, there was an entire deck, and every first-class cabin along both sides had a private veranda. This was the first time for such a feature. These verandas made these ships top draws. Of course, they were favored also for their exceptional Italian cuisine and for their superb Cosulich service. They were two of the very best-run liners of all time."

"They were probably the most successful ships that Italian Line ever owned," added Captain Mario Vespa, who worked for Cosulich in the 1930s. "They were successful before the war but even more successful afterward, in the late 1940s and in the '50s. Tens of thousands of Italian and European immigrants used them after the Second World War for their voyages to North America, to Halifax and to New York. They were strong and very solid and excellent 'sea boats.' They sailed for the Italian Line for an exceptional thirty-seven years."

Vulcania

With her broad, flat stack, the *Vulcania* appears somewhat heavy in this photograph (***above***), dated May 1933. She is seen from the *Conte di Savoia*. [Built by Cantieri Navale Triestino, Monfalcone, Italy, 1928. 23,970 gross tons; 631 feet long; 79 feet wide. Burmeister & Wain diesels, twin screw. Service speed 19 knots. 2,196 passengers (279 first class, 257 second class, 310 third class, 1,350 fourth class).]

The *Vulcania*'s swimming pool (***below***) was one of the most elegant in the fleet. An Italian Line booklet of the 1930s said, "The *Vulcania* . . . companion to the glamorous *Saturnia* . . . as brilliant, as swift and as luxurious. She has all the comforts and the charms of her sisters and varies only in her style of decoration. She has a similar deck of veranda apartments . . . grand stairwells . . . a swimming pool rich with the world's finest marbles and mosaics . . . with steam baths, a small bar and a gallery . . . the gymnasium next door . . . and more than Roman grandeur. She is also a motor ship, driven by the same cool and clean motors."

It concluded, "The rarest of food and wines are perfectly served either in her majestic Dining Salon or the more intimate Grill Room. The Smoking Room of the *Vulcania* suggests Sir Francis Drake and the Spanish Armada . . . a true sea style for a true ship."

Saturnia

The sumptuous grand ballroom aboard the *Saturnia* (**left**) was two decks in height. Italian Line literature in the mid-1930s said of it, "The richness of this Grand Ball Room provides a perfect setting for the full social life of charming people." [Built by Cantiere Navale Triestino, Monfalcone, 1927. 23,940 gross tons; 632 feet long; 79 feet wide. Burmeister & Wain diesels, twin screw. Service speed 19 knots. 2,197 passengers (279 first class, 257 second class, 309 third class, 1,352 fourth class).]

A closer, more detailed view (**below**) of the far end of the grand ballroom onboard the *Saturnia*.

Typical of the opulent public spaces on the *Saturnia* was this grand staircase (**opposite**) with its lush carpet.

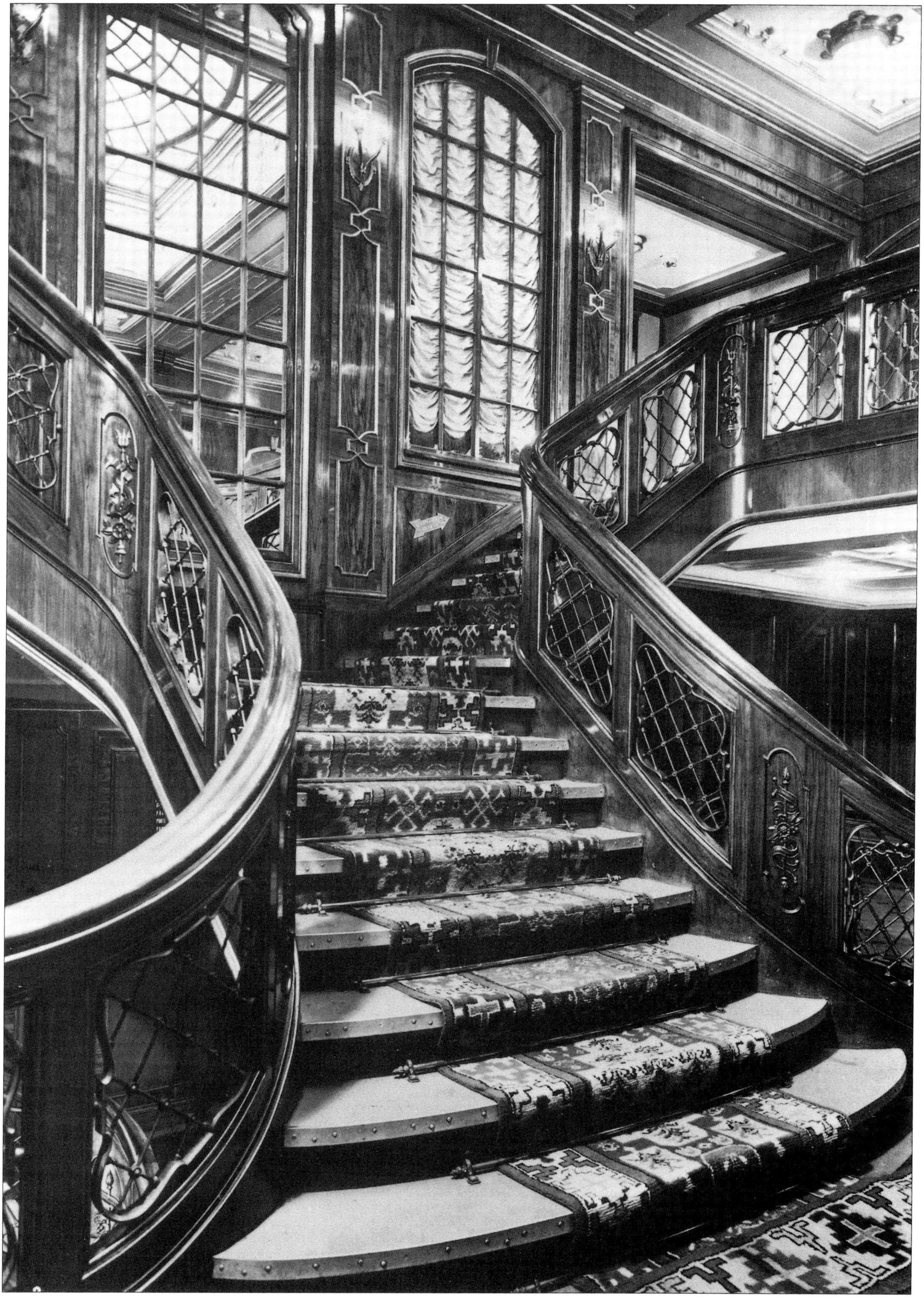

Passengers enjoy the upper, outer decks of the *Saturnia* *(above)*. Italian Line called itself the "Lido Deck Route to Europe." The advertising copy read, "At a glance you discover the secret of one of the greatest travel pleasures of today. To cross on the sparkling Southern Route . . . and to travel on ships built for sunshine, for dark blue waters, for Riviera life at sea! Once across the Gulf Stream, you discard your topcoat . . . the sun is shining! Everybody is on deck in sport clothes . . . playing or promenading. It makes no difference which vessel . . . each Italian Line ship is a true 'sun ship' . . . offering an added thousand miles of cruising east of Gibraltar at no added cost!"

A first-class stateroom aboard the *Saturnia* in 1937 *(opposite, top)* was priced at $215 per person from New York all the way to the last port in the Adriatic. A sample sailing for the ship departed on March 27 of that year, calling at Boston on the following day and then Lisbon seven days later, followed by Gibraltar, Algiers, Naples, Palermo, Patras, and Trieste (fifteen days after New York).

The *Saturnia* and the *Vulcania* were laid up soon after Italy entered World War II in June 1940. In the spring of 1942, they were chartered to the International Red Cross for evacuation voyages out of East Africa. They are seen here at Genoa *(opposite, bottom)* in a wartime gathering of former passenger ships: From left to right, the *Vulcania*, the *Saturnia*, the *Duilio*, and the *Giulio Cesare*.

24 *Classic Motor Liners*

Classic Motor Liners 25

~4~
To More Distant Shores

In the 1930s, from the Italian Line offices at 624 Fifth Avenue in New York City, travelers could book passage to almost any part of the world. Arrangements might include a week or so to Italy aboard the likes of the *Rex* or the *Roma* and then, at Genoa or Naples, continuation was made on a second vessel, surely smaller, but just as comfortable and as well served and fed. The Italian Line maintained links to South America, Africa, the Middle East, the Orient, and Australia.

In 1937, as an example, four liners sailed on a busy schedule to the east coast of South America—to Pernambuco, Bahia, Rio de Janeiro, Santos, sometimes Rio Grande, Montevideo, and Buenos Aires. Genoa to Buenos Aires took seventeen days and cost $19 per person per day in a first-class stateroom. It was $11 per day in second class. That year, the service was run by four large ships—the *Conte Biancamano*, the *Augustus*, the *Neptunia*, and the *Oceania*. To the west coast of South America, via the Caribbean and the Panama Canal to Colombia, Ecuador, Peru, and Chile, the smaller *Orazio* and *Virgilio* sailed almost monthly.

There were a number of routings to Africa. There was the South Africa express service using the *Duilio* and *Giulio Cesare*. Genoa-Capetown took sixteen days and cost $204 in first class. Then there was a separate West African service to such ports as Dakar, Conakry, Takoradi, Accra, and Lagos. Other services went completely around the continent.

The Mid- and Far-Eastern links were, like the African routes, run by Lloyd Triestino, a sister company to the Italian Line through government control. On this run were such liners as the splendid *Victoria* and the sisters *Conte Rosso* and *Conte Verde*. They were routed from Genoa and Naples (as well as Trieste and Venice) to Port Said, Massawa, Aden, Bombay, Colombo, Singapore, Manila, Hong Kong, and Shanghai. The twenty-four-day voyage from Genoa to Shanghai cost a minimum of $390 in first class.

The Australian service was also run by Lloyd Triestino ships and was shown as going from Genoa and Naples to Port Said, Colombo, Fremantle, Melbourne, and Sydney.

Inter-Mediterranean passenger services were plentiful and included those of the Adriatica Line, Lloyd Triestino, and the Tirrenia Lines. Tirrenia, for example, provided such links as Naples–Palmero, Naples–Malta–Tripoli and Naples–Tripoli–Alexandria. Adriatica ran the so-called "Grand Express" service between Genoa and Naples as well as Trieste and Venice to Alexandria. Genoa to Alexandria took four days, for example, and was shown as $120 per person in a minimum first-class cabin. There were also services to Haifa, Istanbul, and ports along the Black Sea.

After the Second World War, almost all of these passenger services were resumed, mostly with different, newly built tonnage. Until the 1970s you could still visit Italian Line's New York office and book passage by ship to much of the world.

Neptunia and Oceania

These sister ships were very similar looking on the outside to the earlier and larger *Saturnia* and *Vulcania*. The Cosulich Line owners had the two ships built in 1932 for the Italy–South America run. The *Oceania* (**above**) is berthed at Trieste. [Built by Cantieri Riuniti dell'Adriatico, Monfalcone, Italy, 1932. 19,507 gross tons; 590 feet long; 73 feet wide. Fiat diesels, twin screw. Service speed 19 knots. 1,385 passengers (200 cabin class, 685 third class, 500 steerage).]

28 *To More Distant Shores*

Fully integrated into the Italian Line sailing schedules and operations in 1937, the *Neptunia* and the *Oceania* catered to Italian immigrants bound for new lives in Brazil, Uruguay, and Argentina in their third-class and steerage quarters. In cabin class, however, the line catered to businessmen, government officials, the high clergy and tourists sailing between Europe and Latin America. These views show the main lounge (***opposite, top***), the bar-lounge (***opposite, bottom***), and the restaurant in cabin class (***above***). The *Neptunia* and the *Oceania* became troopships in 1940, then ended their careers prematurely, in an amazing twist of fate. Both ships were sunk by a British submarine off the Libyan coast on the same day, September 18, 1941. In all, there were 384 casualties.

Orazio and Virgilio

Navigazione Generale Italiana built two smallish passenger ships for the run from Genoa to the west coast of South America via the Panama Canal. The *Orazio* and the *Virgilio* sailed as far south as Valparaiso. In 1932, both ships were transferred to the new Italian Line, and both later became losses in the war years. The *Orazio* was actually lost before Italy entered the war. On January 21, 1940, while carrying 645 passengers and crew on a voyage from Genoa to Barcelona en route to South America, she caught fire at sea in bad weather. French warships and the Italian liners *Conte Biancamano* and *Colombo* answered her distress calls. In the end, 106 perished. The *Virgilio* (**below**), shown here at Genoa, became a hospital ship soon after Italy entered the war, in June 1940. She was seized by the Nazis just after the Italian capitulation in September 1943, and three months later was badly damaged during the Allied air raids on Toulon, France. In June 1944, her remains were deliberately blown up by the retreating Nazis to block the harbor at Toulon. After the war, those remains were salvaged and then scrapped. [Built by Cantieri ed Officine Meridionali, Baia, Italy, 1928. 11,718 gross tons; 506 feet long; 61 feet wide. Burmeister & Wain diesels, twin screw. Service speed 14 knots. 640 passengers (110 first class, 190 second class, 340 third class).]

Victoria (1931)

From New York, you could book passage on an Italian Line ship to Genoa and then transfer to a luxury ship like the *Victoria* and sail all the way to Shanghai or to Hong Kong. Unquestionably, the finest passenger ship in the Lloyd Triestino fleet of the 1930s was the *Victoria* (*above*). Sleek and handsome, often compared to a large yacht, she had an enviable reputation for high speed, high style, and superb service. By most Europeans and even the British themselves, she was often preferred over the well-known P&O passenger ships. She was a great favorite on the Bombay route as well. [Built by Cantieri Riuniti dell'Adriatico, Monfalcone, Italy, 1931. 13,062 gross tons; 540 feet long; 70 feet wide. Sulzer diesels, quadruple screw. Service speed 20.5 knots. 666 passengers (239 first class, 245 second class, 100 third class, 82 fourth class).]

The first-class quarters on board the *Victoria* were sumptuous. The first class bar (*right*), by architect Gustavo Pulitzer Finali, was designed in high Art Deco style. Noted as the fastest motor ship afloat (with a maximum speed of 23.26 knots), the *Victoria* was another casualty of the Second World War. On January 24, 1942, while on a voyage from Taranto to Tripoli, she sank in the Gulf of Sidra, off the coast of Libya, after an attack by British aircraft.

To More Distant Shores

Esperia

One of the largest Mediterranean passenger liners of her time, the *Esperia* (***above***) was launched at the end of the First World War, in 1918, and then completed in March 1921. She sailed from Genoa to Alexandria, then back north to Venice and Trieste before returning to Egypt and finally home to Genoa. Built for Societa Italiana di Servizi Marittimi of Naples, she was transferred in 1932 to Lloyd Triestino and then, in 1937, to the Adriatica Line. She was a casualty of the Second World War, sunk on August 20, 1941, while in a convoy from Italy to North Africa. Thirty-one of those on board perished. [Built by Societa Ersercicio Bacini, Riva Trigoso, Italy, 1918–21. 11,398 gross tons; 528 feet long; 61 feet wide. Steam turbines, twin screw. Service speed 19 knots. 479 passengers (205 first class, 118 second class, 56 third class, 100 steerage).]

A noted passenger aboard the *Esperia*: Baroness Thyssen-Bornemisza (***left***) disembarks at Genoa.

32   *To More Distant Shores*

Colombo

This ship had a long, diverse history. Launched in October 1915 as the *San Gennaro*, she was soon laid up owing to the First World War. Ordered by the Sicula Americana Line, she was in fact completed in 1917, but as a cargo ship for Transoceanica, a subsidiary of Navigazione Generale Italiana. She then sailed for a brief time under charter to the British. In 1921, she was rebuilt as a passenger ship and renamed *Colombo*. At first used on the Mediterranean–New York run, she later was rerouted to the west coast of South America, sailing from Genoa to Valparaiso via Panama. In 1932, she passed into the ownership of the Italian Line and was later used as a troop transport to East Africa. In 1937, she was again transferred, going to Lloyd Triestino for Genoa–Suez–Massawa–Djibouti service. In this view at Massawa, the *Colombo* (**below**) forms a backdrop as members of the Italian navy pass in review before Prince Eugenio of Savoy, the Duke of Ancona.

On April 8, 1941, when the Italian naval port of Massawa in Eritrea was taken by the British, the *Colombo* was deliberately blown up by her Italian crew to avoid capture. In 1949, her wreckage was salvaged and then scrapped. [Built by Palmers Shipbuilding & Iron Company Limited, Jarrow-on-Tyne, England, 1915–17. 11,762 gross tons; 536 feet long; 64 feet wide. Steam quadruple expansion engines, twin screw. Service speed 16 knots. 2,800 passengers (100 first class, 700 second class, 2,000 third class).]

Heavily loaded with Italian troops, the *Colombo* (***above***) departs for East Africa in 1935. In that same year the Cosulich Line freighter *Atlanta* (***below***), refitted as a troopship, sails for East African waters.

~5~
Floating Palaces

"The *Rex* and the *Conte di Savoia* were among the very finest ships of the 1930s, certainly the very best that Italy could produce and possibly the two finest, most famous Italian luxury liners ever," said Vito Sardi, a steward aboard the *Rex* in 1939–40. "They were big and very powerful, great works of engineering and, of course, decorated in the highest style. In every way, they were Italy's floating palaces."

The high spirits and optimism of the late 1920s led shipping companies to plan for, among other things, larger and more lavish ocean liners—in fact, the biggest that had ever been seen. Size mattered a great deal. In New York, for example, the building of the great skyscrapers echoed this trend. The 77-story Chrysler Building of 1929 led to the 102-story Empire State Building two years later. On the seas, the French *Normandie* (1935) was the first ocean liner to exceed 1,000 feet in length and to surpass the 75,000-ton mark. The previous record-holder was Britain's *Majestic*, at 950 feet and 56,500 tons. Internally, the design of these new ships was spectacular and increasingly innovative—with stylized lounges, extravagant suites and staterooms, a full tennis court on the top deck (aboard the *Empress of Britain*), resortlike lido decks (the *Rex* and the *Conte di Savoia*), and a winter garden complete with caged birds and live greenery (the *Normandie*). There were also indoor pools and health clubs, a bowling alley on one ship, flower and chocolate shops, and even a men's tailor on another. But it was great speed, the sense of mechanical power, that often meant the most to the greatest number of passengers, created more newspaper headlines, and produced the most spirited goodwill. Winning the coveted Blue Ribbon for the fastest speed across the Atlantic was still very much a matter of national prestige. Great Britain had held it for twenty-two years, from 1907 until 1929, with that glorious Cunarder, the *Mauretania*. She was a 32,000-tonner.

It was the Germans who started a new "race" for ocean liner distinctions in the late twenties. Despite their inglorious losses in the First World War, they—the North German Lloyd in particular—had recovered sufficiently to order twin 35,000-ton liners in 1925. But the pair was soon redesigned to reach the 50,000-ton mark and to be given very powerful machinery. Named *Bremen* and *Europa*, these ships would sail on a "dual maiden voyage" planned so that both would break the Atlantic speed record and thus take the honors from the British. In fact, the *Bremen* snatched the trophy first, in July 1929, with an average of 27.83 knots between Cherbourg and New York's Ambrose Light, beating the *Mauretania's* 26.6 knots. The *Europa*, delayed by a shipyard fire, arrived a year later and established a new record, 27.91 knots.

In 1931, Britain responded with Canadian Pacific's 42,300-ton *Empress of Britain*—a magnificent ship in every way, but no speed champion. Italy, never a contender before, emerged a year later with the *Rex* and then the *Conte di Savoia*. The 51,000-ton *Rex* took the record in August 1933 at 28.92 knots and held it for nearly two years, until May 1935 and the arrival of the even more powerful *Normandie*.

The extraordinary, innovative, quite magical *Normandie*, at nearly 80,000 tons, was the ship, like no other, that pulled out all the stops. "Floating fantasy," said one observer. A vessel of exceptional, often startling decorative style—Lalique lighting fixtures, Aubusson carpets, Dupas glass panels, every first-class stateroom in a different decor—she was also a ship of great might. The *Normandie* took the Blue Ribbon on her maiden voyage in the spring of 1935, with an average speed of 29.98 knots. The glorious, ever-beloved *Queen Mary* regained it for Britain in August 1936 at 30.63 knots and then, after a few more contests with the French Line flagship, won it permanently. The Blue Ribbon went to the brilliant *United States* in 1952. She would be the last luxury liner to fly the pennant.

Mussolini himself, his government, and in fact all of Italy were rightly very proud of the *Rex* and the *Conte di Savoia*. They were the first superliners for the Italians and the first of their size to serve the Mediterranean. Public relations officers worked hard to give them a special image. Suggesting the glories of a southern European vacation, they were dubbed the "Rivieras afloat"—the beginning of the so-called floating resorts. They were popular ships, prompting at least thoughts of a third superliner by the late thirties, along with plans to rebuild and re-engine the slightly smaller *Augustus* and *Roma* as improved running mates to this larger pair. In fact, the *Rex* and the *Conte di Savoia* were not great moneymakers. The Depression was of course damaging, and then their "sunny, southern Mediterranean route" still did not have quite the allure, the pure tradition of the northern route to and from Europe—through the likes of Southampton, Cherbourg, or Le Havre. But the money the ships lost didn't really matter—the Italian government was quite willing to subsidize such prestigious liners.

They were the last superliners to continue commercial sailings in and out of New York—into the spring of 1940, long after others had ceased (the *Queen Mary*, for example, was already in somber gray and running heroic troop voyages). The *Rex* and the *Conte di Savoia* would become casualties of war all too soon. Laid up and kept out of sight by the Nazis after the Italian capitulation the *Conte di Savoia* was set afire to avoid escape or capture. She burnt out on September 11, 1943. A year later, the Allied commanders decided that the *Rex* must be destroyed as a cruel symbol of defeat to the already ravaged Italians. Nearly 125 rockets were fired on the lonely, anchored ship, lying south of Trieste. She burned, then capsized. After the war, the only notations for these exceptional Italian superliners, barely fifteen years old at the time, were details of their demolition—the final scrapping, the exhumation of their remains.

Rex

Navigazione Generale Italiana were delighted with the success of the sisters *Roma* and *Augustus*, and this prompted the company to think of an even bigger vessel. The Italian government, itself thinking of the positive national image created by an extravagant ocean liner, assured a generous construction loan as well as an operating subsidy, supposedly given to transport mail and rated according to the ship's speed. Both the company and the government agreed that this new liner must not only be beautifully decorated, a floating symbol of Italian style, art, and history, but capable of wresting the Blue Ribbon from Germany's *Bremen* and *Europa*.

King Victor Emmanuel III and Queen Elena attended the naming ceremony and launching of this new Italian supership, on August 1, 1931 *(above)*. It pleased the royal couple that the name *Rex* had been selected. It was, in fact, a deliberate effort on the part of Premier Benito Mussolini to win further favor among Italy's royalist factions. The previous suggestion to name the ship *Guglielmo Marconi* was abandoned by the premier himself. At the launching, officials of both NGI as well as the Ansaldo shipyard spoke optimistically of winning the Blue Ribbon within a year or so.

Construction, which had been accelerated, sped forth with even greater urgency. [Built by Ansaldo Shipyards, Genoa, Italy, 1932. 51,062 gross tons; 880 feet long; 96 feet wide. Steam turbines, quadruple screw. Service speed 28 knots. 2,358 passengers (604 first class, 378 second class, 410 tourist class, 966 third class).]

Premier Mussolini attended a gala luncheon and toured the completed *Rex* just hours before her maiden departure from Genoa, on September 27, 1932 *(opposite)*. Dressed in colorful flags, to the sounds of saluting horns and sirens, and with a passenger list of international celebrities that included New York City's Mayor James J. Walker, the liner sailed on what was intended to be her record-breaking crossing. She called at Villefranche and then headed west. But suddenly, while approaching Gibraltar, fate overtook the festive occasion: serious engine problems all but crippled the brand-new flagship. The embarrassed Italian Line reported that repairs would be made in hours, that the delay would be a minor one. Closer inspection, however, found far more serious problems. There would be a three-day delay at the British colony. Many first-class passengers, including Mayor Walker, grew impatient and left the liner. The Italians were mortified.

36 Floating Palaces

Floating Palaces   37

38 *Floating Palaces*

The *Rex* eventually continued her crossing to New York, then had further mechanical problems. Once at New York, she was forced to cancel her eastbound maiden sailing, relying on auxiliary power from a floating railway tender while awaiting parts from subsequent inbound Italian liners. The Blue Ribbon had to wait. The *Rex* finally captured her intended prize, from the *Bremen*, almost a year later, in August 1933. She crossed with a recorded average speed of 28.92 knots against the German liner's 28.51 knots. The passage between Gibraltar and Ambrose Light was thus reduced to 4 days, 13 hours, and 58 minutes. This record would hold until the *Normandie*'s arrival in May 1935.

Floating Palaces 39

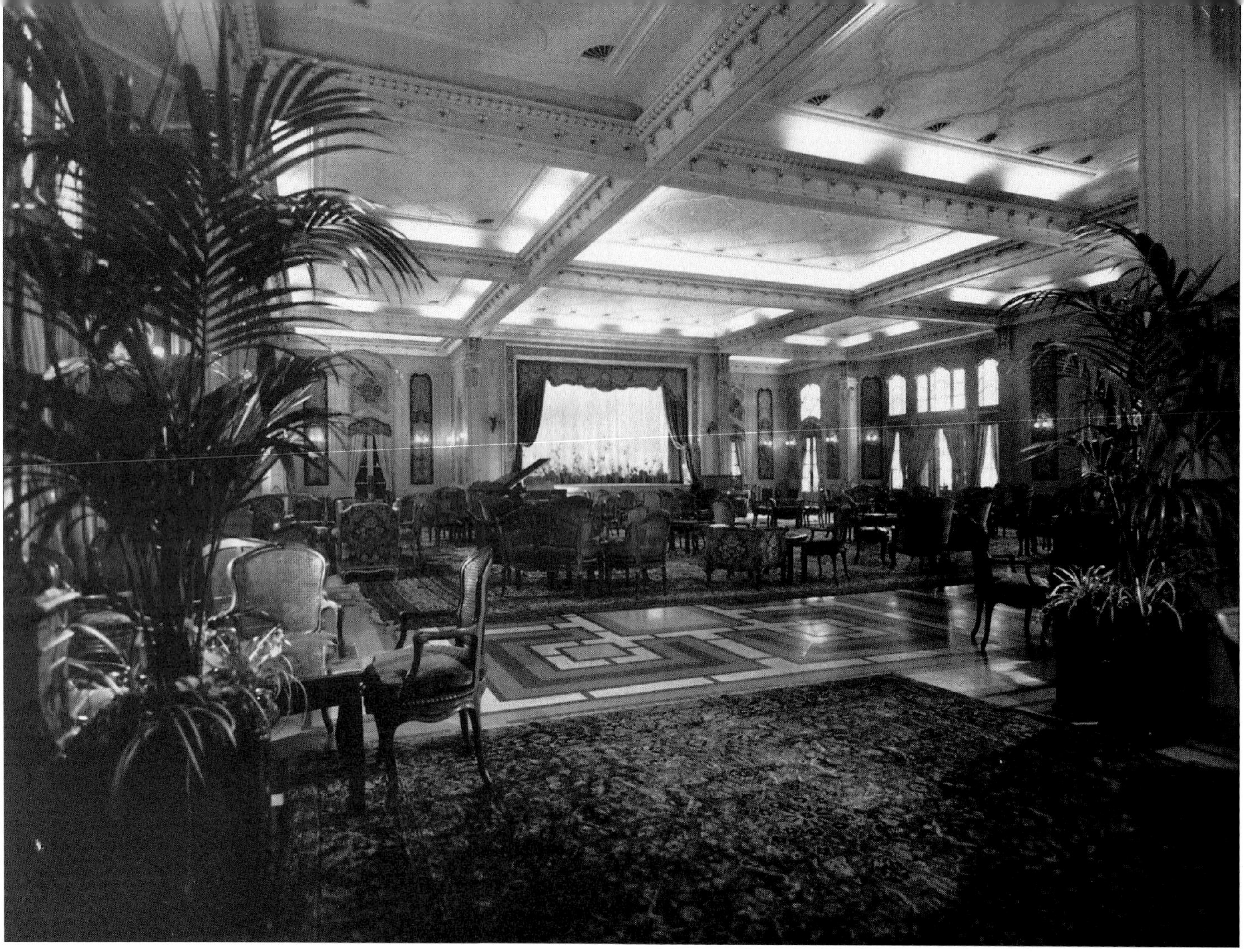

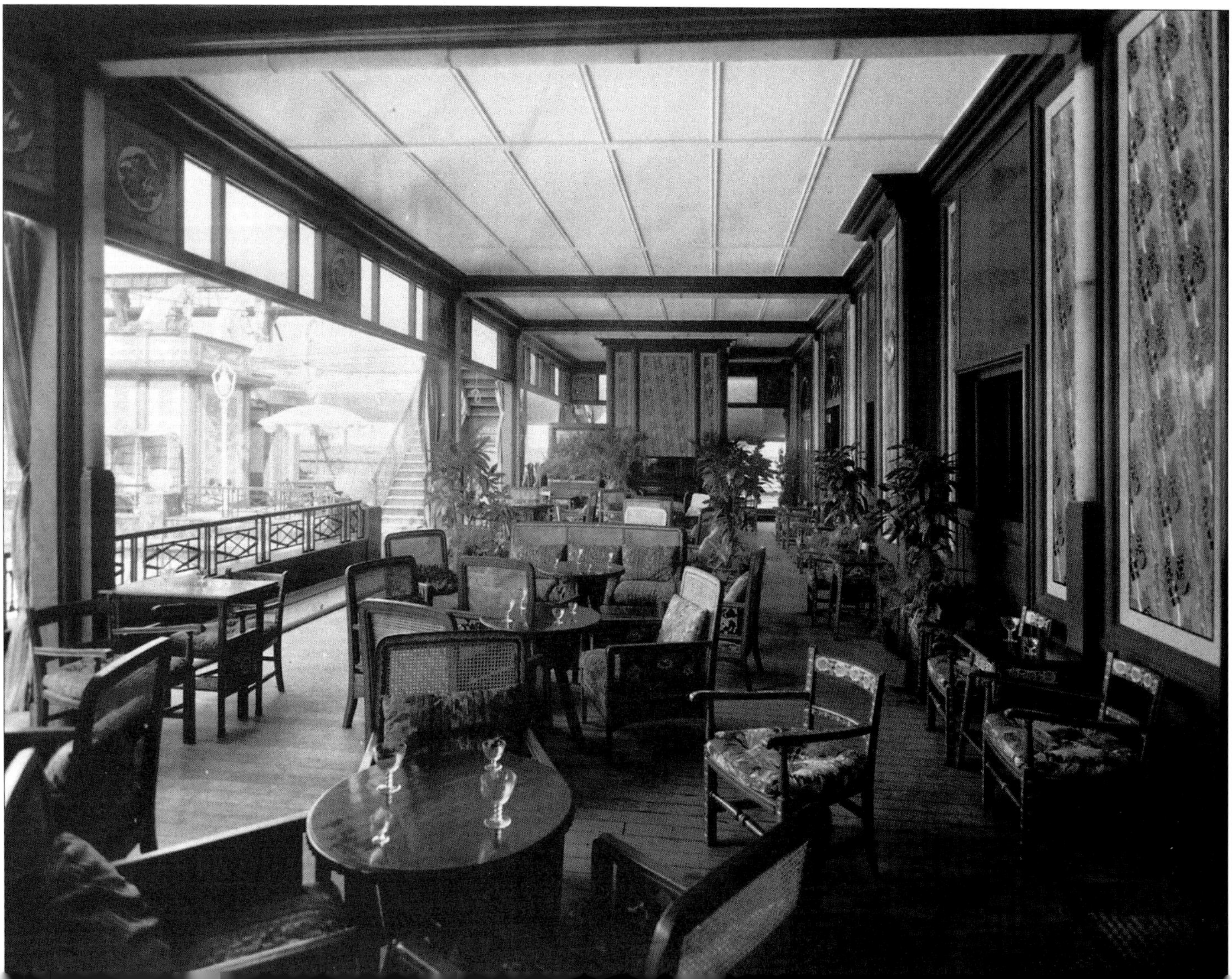

The *Rex* was soon acclaimed as one of the world's most beautiful ships. The impressive grand ballroom (***opposite, top***) also served as a fully equipped theater for entertainment, concerts, and the screening of films. The glorious first-class veranda (***opposite, bottom***) faced onto the lido deck and the tiled swimming pool.

The first-class dining room aboard the *Rex* (***above***) was the pride of the Italian Line. Advertisements said of the *Rex*: "She has caught the beauty and art of Italy's 18th century. The *Rex* is regally furnished with the glories of sunny palaces . . . original tapestries and damask of the period, painting, exquisite wrought iron in great halls throughout the ship. But the artistic glories of the 18th century are enhanced by the conveniences and luxuries of the 20th century's contribution to shipbuilding."

    Another description read, "Good cuisine and good music follow no boundary lines, and the Italian Line is the Esperanto for good living and good food to those who have traveled the world. Menus on ships like the *Rex* need merely to serve as reminders and for suggestions. The world's finest cuisine . . . and its best dishes . . . are your menu . . . and all served by English-speaking stewards . . . as the swift liner slips along the sunny lane of the Gulf Stream to the Mediterranean!"

Floating Palaces

First-class stateroom number 35 aboard the *Rex* (**above**) included a private veranda. In the early 1930s it was priced at $270 per person for the seven-day crossing from New York to Naples or the eight days to Villefranche and Genoa.

Once each year, the *Rex* took its turn in the graving dock at Genoa for general maintenance, survey, and repairs (**opposite, top**). On one occasion, during a voyage from New York, the mighty ship was tossed about in heavy seas for a full twelve hours. One crewman died and dozens of passengers were injured. In March 1937, during high winds, the liner slammed into New York's Pier 88 while undocking (**opposite, bottom**).

42   *Floating Palaces*

Floating Palaces 43

Italian Line advertisements called their ships "the Royal Family of the Seven Seas." In a view *(below)* dated September 27, 1932, five passenger ships are together at Genoa: From left to right, the *Vienna* of Lloyd Triestino, the Italian Line's *Rex*, the *Conte di Savoia*, the *Conte Grande*, and the *Victoria*, also Lloyd Triestino.

After September 1939, the *Rex* and her Italian Line fleetmates were among the last foreign-flag passenger ships to remain in transatlantic service, supposedly as a symbol of Italy's continued neutrality. Service finally ended the following spring, just as the political situation and the safety of the ships at sea could no longer be guaranteed. The *Rex* was laid-up for security reasons at Bari, on the Adriatic coast. On August 15, following a change in plans, she was towed to Trieste. She would never sail again. Various wartime reports hinted that she was to be rebuilt as an aircraft carrier, similar to the plans for the *Roma* and the *Augustus*, or at least to be used as a high-capacity troopship. Worst of all, there was word that the Nazis planned to use her as a blockade to Venice harbor, sinking her deliberately to thwart the Allies. None of these plans came to pass. Instead, on September 8, 1944, the anchored liner was sighted by Royal Air Force bombers and was hit with no less than 123 rockets. She burst into flames from end to end and, on the following day, rolled over and sank in the shallow waters of Capodistria, in the Gulf of Muggia, south of Trieste *(opposite, top)*.

At the end of the war, initial studies were made in the hope of salvaging the *Rex*, but she was damaged beyond economic repair *(opposite, bottom)*. She was declared a complete loss. Scrapping on the spot began in 1947, but the final pieces were not removed until June 1958. The Italians would never again build a faster passenger liner.

44 Floating Palaces

45

46 *Floating Palaces*

Conte di Savoia

When Lloyd Sabaudo firmly decided, in the late 1920s, to build a new passenger liner of great size and superior decoration, they were not interested in record-breaking speed. Quite simply, they left that distinction to the rival Navigazione Generale Italiana and its new flagship, a vessel that would become the *Rex*. But the new Sabaudo superliner (***opposite***) captured just as much interest and attention from Premier Mussolini and his government. [Built by Cantieri Riuniti dell'Adriatico, Trieste, Italy, 1932. 48,502 gross tons; 814 feet long; 96 feet wide. Steam turbines, quadruple screw. Service speed 27 knots. 2,200 passengers (500 first class, 366 second class, 412 tourist class, 922 third class).]

The *Conte di Savoia* was christened on October 28, 1931, by the Princess of Piedmont, the Italian equivalent to Britain's Princess of Wales. The ship's name was selected, again personally by Mussolini, to honor and impress the ruling House of Savoy and to win over other royal factions. The original choice had been *Dux*, which was thought to be a more suitable companion name to *Rex*. But then this was changed to *Conte Azzuro* before the third and final selection was made. Workmen put on the final touches (***above***) before she was launched with a full weight of 18,730 tons.

Floating Palaces

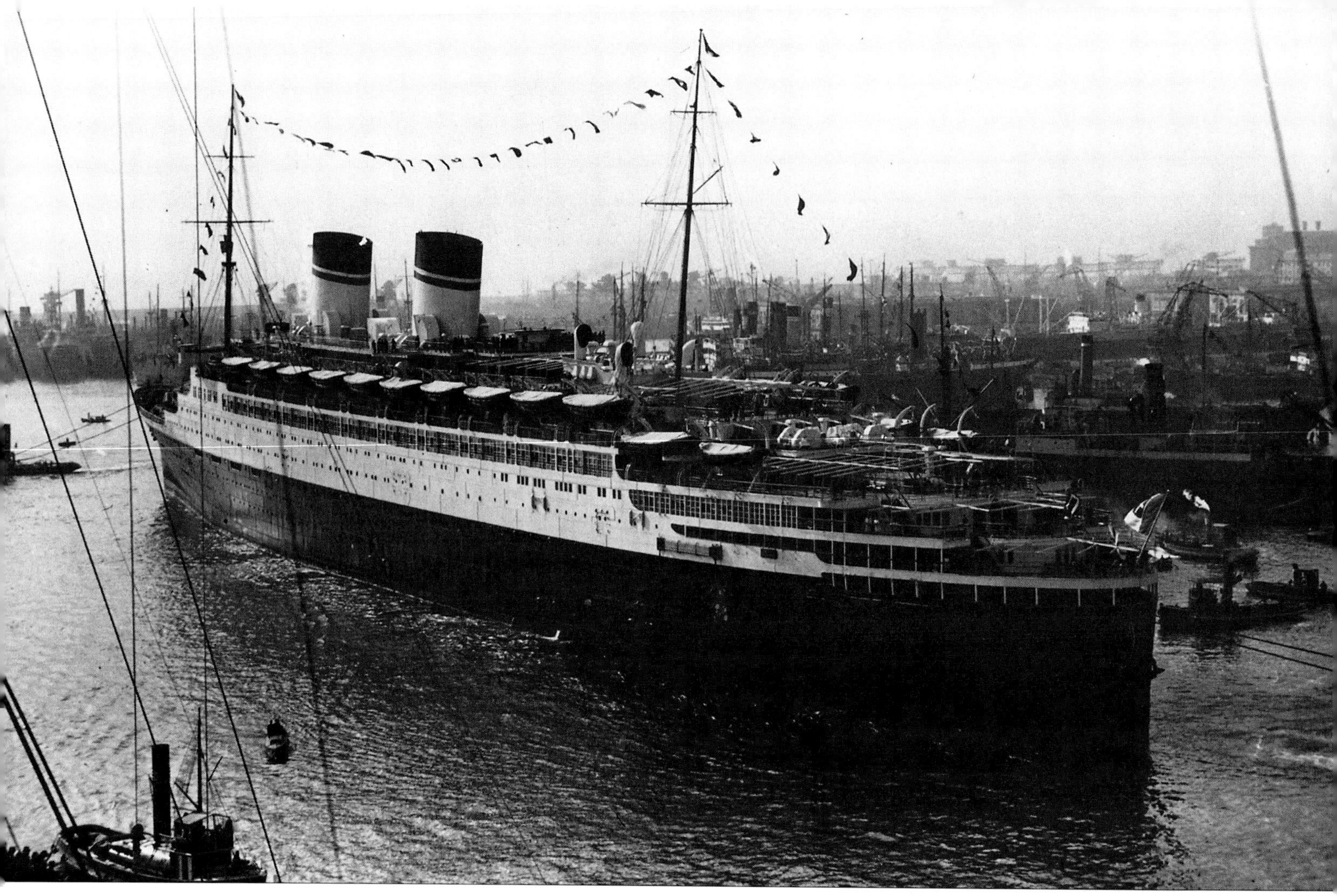

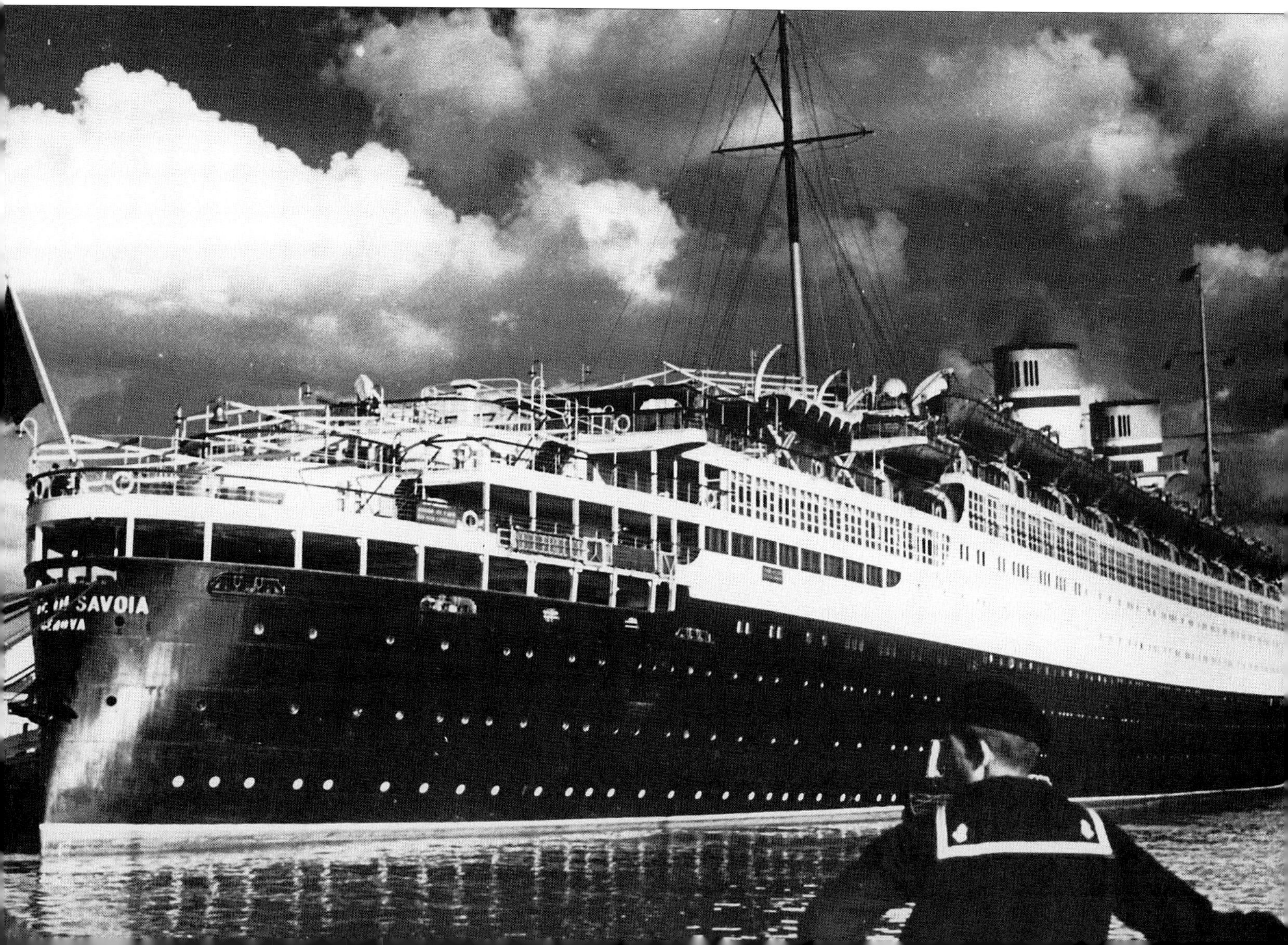
DI SAVOIA

Early in November 1932 the *Conte di Savoia* went off on her official sea trials, achieving a top speed of 29.5 knots on one occasion. On the 30th of that month, she left Genoa (***opposite, top***) on her maiden voyage to New York. While coming a mere two months after the *Rex*, this second Italian supership nevertheless attracted great attention and interest. All seemed to pass quite well until, some 900 miles west of the North American shore, an outlet valve below the waterline jammed and subsequently blew a very worrisome hole in the side of the hull. In a matter of minutes, the ship began to flood. Reports were relayed to the bridge but sensibly kept from the otherwise happy passengers. It was calculated that the ship could sink—on her maiden voyage, no less—in as few as five hours. Fortunately, the ship's engineers and crew members were resourceful. One near-superhuman seaman succeeded in filling the open hole with cement. The *Conte di Savoia* was out of danger. Later, when full reports reached the passengers, a good-sized booty was passed to the heroic sailor.

Since both the *Rex* and the *Conte di Savoia* (***opposite, bottom***) had difficult maiden voyages, suspicions were aroused that their construction had been rushed to completion as a result of pressure from Mussolini himself. In contrast to other big European liners, these two Italians were completed in less than two years. In any event, with the problems settled, they soon began to enjoy otherwise trouble-free commercial careers.

While the *Rex* was noted as a Blue Ribbon champion, the *Conte di Savoia* was known as the "roll-less ship." She was the first major liner and the very first ship of any type on the Atlantic run to have the new gyro stabilizer system (***above***). It was a balancing arrangement that predated the fin stabilizer design, which was perfected for passenger ships in the 1950s. The stabilizers aboard this Italian liner were widely publicized as having the ability to reduce the rolling as well as the pitching of the ship. In reality, however, the system was oversold by the Italians and their exuberant press efforts of 1932–33. While the gyro proved successful to some extent, it could not be used, for example, on westbound crossings because prevailing winds might seriously jeopardize the ship's balance and therefore her safety. In fact, passengers aboard the *Conte di Savoia* were often quite surprised to have her rolling and tossing about just like any "ordinary" transatlantic liner.

Floating Palaces 49

From a design viewpoint, the *Conte di Savoia* was a tour de force of Italian decorative splendor. The immense Colonna Hall (*above*), a magnificent space of rich marbles inspired by the Gallery of the Colonna Palace in Rome, was perhaps her finest and therefore best-remembered public space. There was a great ceiling with murals, impressive entranceways, and towering statues on pedestals lining the port and starboard sides. Certainly, this decor contrasted sharply to the more angular, sleek Art Deco style aboard the likes of the subsequent *Normandie* and *Queen Mary*. The Princess Gallery (*left*), which served as a promenade of sorts that connected various public rooms, was noticeably Deco in style. It was designed by Gustavo Pulitzer Finali.

"The circular first-class bar aboard the *Conte di Savoia* (*opposite*) is ingeniously devised and decorated," said an Italian Line press release.

Floating Palaces 51

The card room *(left, top)* on the *Conte di Savoia* was decorated in the sleek simplicity of 1930s Deco style. "Bright, modern art glows with deft lighting in the brilliant dining salon aboard the *Conte di Savoia*," said one lavish Italian Line booklet entitled "The Mild Southern Route to Europe." This first-class space *(left, middle)* was another fine work of Gustavo Pulitzer Finali. In 1937, a twin-bedded first-class stateroom *(left, bottom)* was priced at $550 per person for a round-trip voyage from New York to the Mediterranean.

Sailing day from Genoa aboard the *Conte di Savoia* *(opposite)*. As the celebrities board the ship as crowds gathered, officials are out in force, and the Movietone cameras are perched atop the trucks to record the event.

Floating Palaces 53

Transatlantic crossings were hardly short of diversions. As a publicity piece read, "Daytime should be spent on the topmost part of the ship . . . a broad and long expanse of deck . . . surrounding a large, brightly tiled pool filled with crystal sea water. Around it, gay loungers in bathing suits and beach pajamas . . . some stretching out on soft, white towels to catch the sun's warm rays . . . others sitting around tables under gay umbrellas sipping a beverage between moves at backgammon. Now and then a plunge in the refreshing pool . . . then back to an engrossing best seller in a wicker chair. And at night . . . the brightly colored festoons of light add to the silvery gleam of the moon. The pool looks even more inviting, brightened by the pastel tints of the underwater lights. Some dance under the smiling stars to the tunes of a compelling dance orchestra. The day on an Italian liner can be a long and happy one!" These views show the dance band in the Colonna Hall *(above)* and that great shipboard pastime: mechanical horse races *(below)*.

Celebrity passengers aboard the *Conte di Savoia*—Crown Prince Umberto *(opposite, top)* at Naples in May 1934, and Queen Victoria Eugenia of Spain *(opposite, bottom)*, third from the right in the Colonna Hall on a voyage in September 1936.

Floating Palaces 55

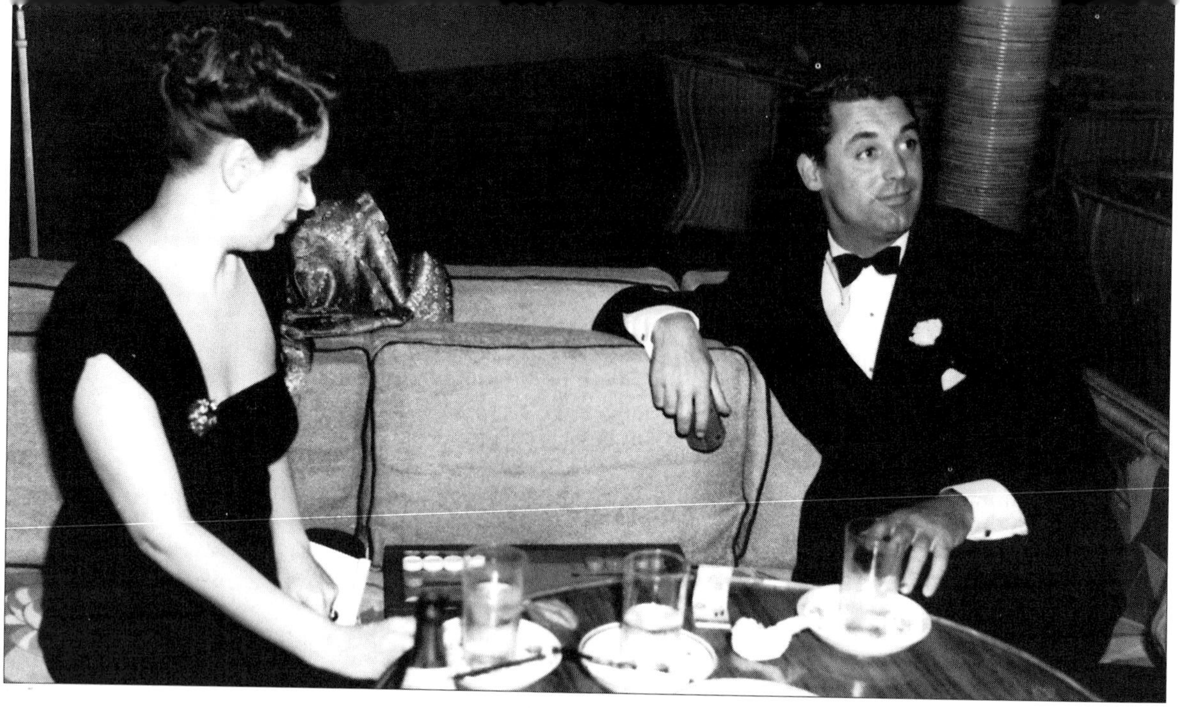

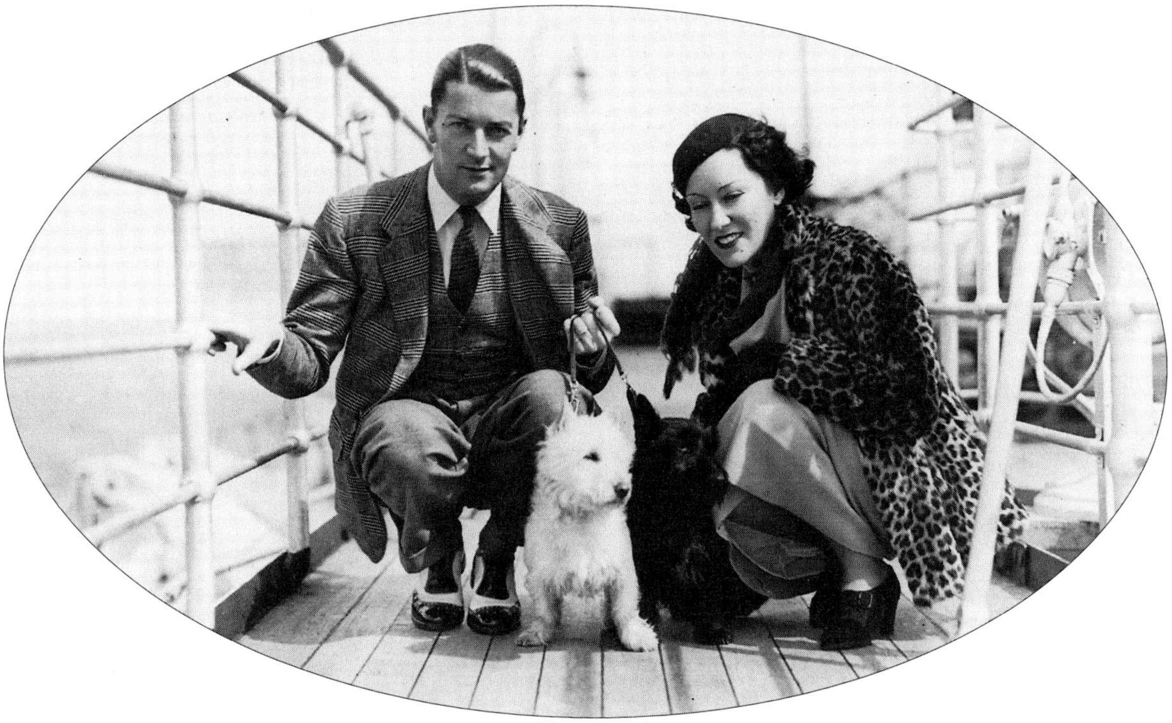

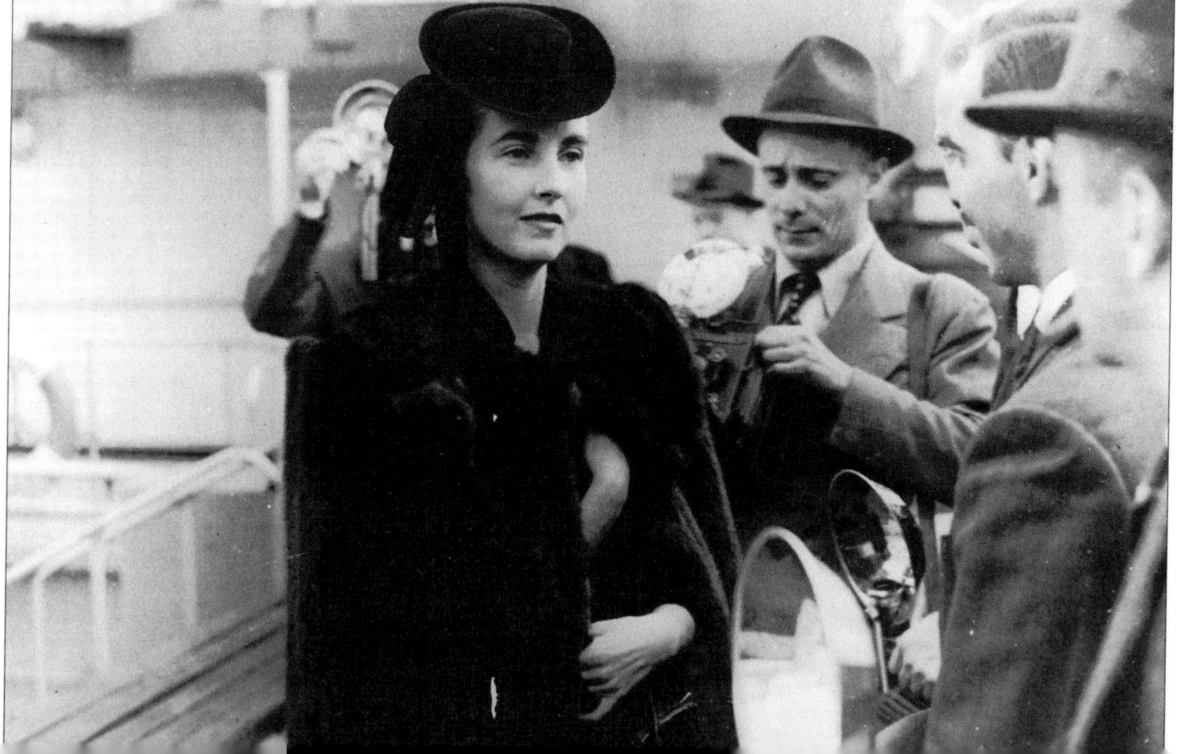

Other celebrity passengers in the late 1930s included Cary Grant (*opposite, top*), Gloria Swanson (*opposite, middle*), and Barbara Hutton (*opposite, bottom*), heiress to the Woolworth fortune.

Two harbor views at Genoa: one from the cliffside Miramar Hotel (*above*) showing (from left to right) the *Augustus*, the *Esquilino* (used on the Italy–Australia run), the *Conte di Savoia*, and the *Rex*. In the opposite direction (from left to right), there are the *Rex*, the *Conte di Savoia*, and the *Conte Grande* (*below*).

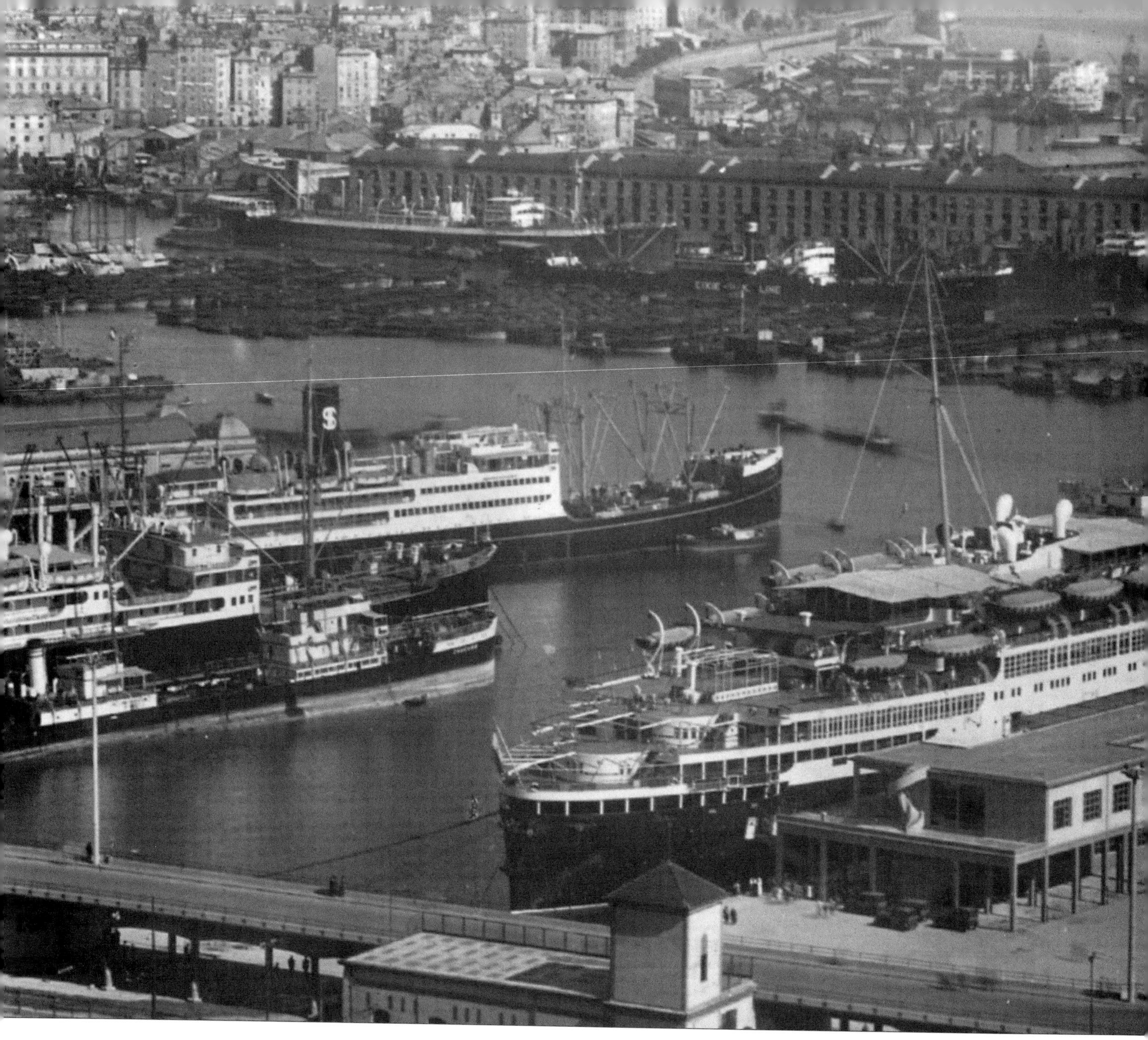

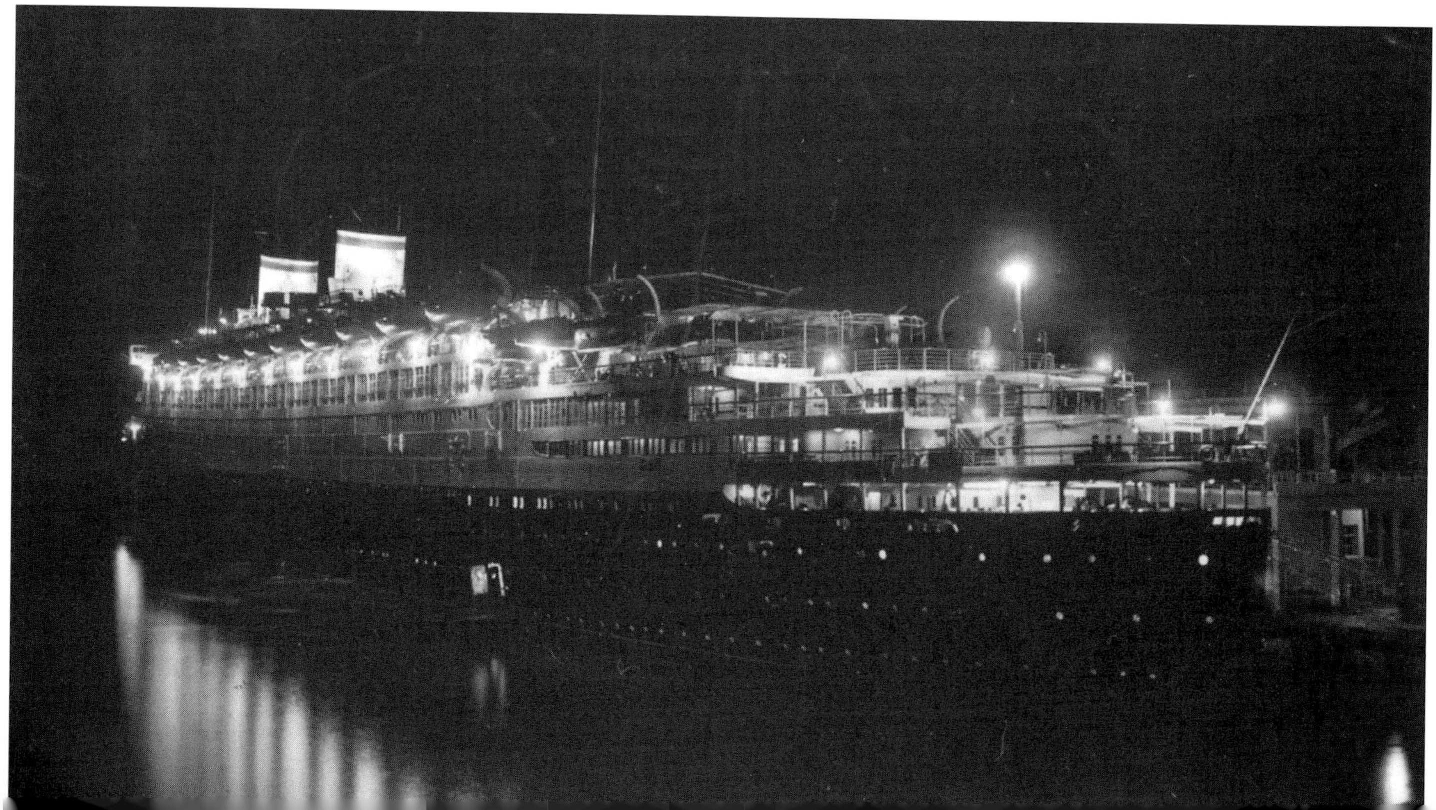

The *Conte di Savoia* (**left**) continued her Atlantic crossings, along with the *Rex*, until the spring of 1940. At the time of her final New York sailing, the Italian Line announced that "both ships will resume their Mediterranean crossings in September, when the war is over." She was sent to the Adriatic and laid up close to Malamocco, near Venice (**opposite, bottom**). Rumors suggested that she too might be rebuilt as an aircraft carrier.

On September 11, 1943, the Nazis ordered that the laid-up *Conte di Savoia* be set afire to prevent its escape or its capture by the Allies. She burnt out completely and then sank in shallow waters. The seriously damaged hull of the *Conte di Savoia* (**below**) was raised on October 16, 1945, and some thought was given to rebuilding her. One design, considered the most likely at the time, showed her as a one-class immigrant ship with 2,500 all-third-class berths. She would have been used on the Italy-South America route. But there were major obstacles: a shortage of rebuilding materials, a shortage of adequate shipyards, and, perhaps most of all, a shortage of money. By 1950, the idea was abandoned and the hulk sold to local scrappers at Monfalcone.

~6~
Rebirth and Restoration

"President Alcide de Gasperi went to see President Truman in 1946 and personally asked for the return of the four Italian liners that were in wartime American hands. He also asked for many Liberty ships," according to Maurizio Eliseo. "There were rumors that the Americans were going to sell the motor liners *Saturnia* and *Vulcania* to the Soviets. Soviet agents had actually inspected them. It was not at all certain that these ships were going to be returned to Italy. The other pair, the *Conte Biancamano* and the *Conte Grande*, were actually 'abandoned' by the Italian Line. The company even let their insurance lapse. These ships were laid up after the war, and their futures uncertain."

President de Gasperi's pleas succeeded. The four passenger liner-troopships were returned to the Italians—the *Saturnia* and the *Vulcania* in December 1946, the *Conte Biancamano* and the *Conte Grande* in the following summer. The first two were restored to much of their prewar splendor—heavy Baroque, richly ornate, period stylings. But changes were made as well. On board the *Saturnia*, for example, her prewar capacity of 2,197 was reduced to 1,370. The *Conte Biancamano* and *Conte Grande* had been so heavily gutted and then rebuilt as troopships by the Americans that they became virtually new ships during their refurbishing in the late '40s. Their passenger quarters were the first examples of "Italian modern" to appear.

The style met with acclaim and was followed on subsequent new liners like the *Augustus*, the *Giulio Cesare*, the *Andrea Doria*, and the *Cristoforo Colombo*, and even on board Lloyd Triestino's first postwar liners, the *Australia*, the *Neptunia*, and the *Oceania*.

After rather quick refits, the motor ships *Saturnia* and *Vulcania* returned to commercial service in January and in July 1947, respectively. They sailed on the express run between Naples, Genoa, Cannes, Gibraltar, and New York. The twin-funnel near-sisters *Conte Grande* and *Conte Biancamano* followed at six-month intervals—the former in July 1949, the latter in November 1949. They went back on the South American run—to Rio de Janeiro, Santos, Montevideo, and Buenos Aires. Months later, in March 1950, the *Conte Biancamano* was needed on the New York trade and so went north to assist the overbooked *Saturnia* and *Vulcania*. Out of the ashes and the rubble and the destruction of the Second World War, the Italians had four luxury liners on their two principal services to the Americas.

The company also added six large combination passenger-cargo ships in 1947–49. These ships, such as the *Paolo Toscanelli*, reopened service to the west coast of South America, sailing from Genoa all the way to Valparaiso, Chile.

Following the Italian surrender to the Allies in 1943, the laid-up *Saturnia* was reactivated and quickly made for an Allied port on September 8th. Immediately, she was seized by the Americans and assigned to the U.S. Navy for use as a troop transport. In January 1945, she began a six-month conversion to the hospital ship *Frances Y. Slanger* (*above*), named for the first American nurse to die in the Second World War. But the ship's hospital duties were rather shortlived—she was decommissioned from this work in November 1945. She was then refitted and sailed under the U.S. Army Transport Service until the following June. Again, she was laid up, with a possible sale or transfer to the Soviets, until formally returned to the Italians on December 1, 1946. Similarly, the *Vulcania* fled after the Italian capitulation. She left on September 8, 1943, and within a month was in American hands and sailing as a troopship. She is shown, still in gray wartime coloring, on the south side of New York's Pier 90 in the winter of 1945–46 (*below*). Cunard Line's *Queen Elizabeth* is just across the rooftop. She was finally returned to the Italians on December 14, 1946.

Rebirth and Restoration 61

62 Rebirth and Restoration

A rainy afternoon in March 1948 makes for a moody setting as the *Saturnia* departs from New York City's Pier 84 *(opposite, top)*. After the Second World War, Italian Line used that West 44th Street berth along Manhattan's West Side until late 1963, when they moved to Cunard's former terminal, Pier 90, at West 50th Street.

Postwar splendor: the first-class main lounge aboard the *Saturnia* *(opposite, bottom)*. From 1947 until 1953, she and her sister ship *Vulcania* maintained Italian Line's express run between Naples, Genoa, and New York. But once the brand-new *Andrea Doria* and *Cristoforo Colombo* were being readied, the two older ships went back to their longer, prewar services. They were scheduled for five- and six-week round-trip voyages: Trieste, Venice, Dubrovnik, Patras, Messina and/or Palermo, Naples, Gibraltar, Lisbon, Halifax (westbound only), and finally New York. They often returned via Boston (one day after New York), then Ponta Delgada in the Azores, Lisbon, Gibraltar, Palermo, Naples, Patras, Venice, and Trieste.

The furniture has a strong Asian tone in this late-1940s view of the first-class gallery aboard the *Vulcania* *(right)*. First-class swimming pools, like the one aboard the *Saturnia* *(below)*, were prized amenities for those often very warm crossings to and from the Mediterranean as well as for the stays in port. Neither ship had air-conditioning and so the temperature in the interior areas, especially in the lower, tourist-class spaces, might soar to 100 degrees in high summer.

Rebirth and Restoration 63

64   *Rebirth and Restoration*

The *Saturnia* and the *Vulcania* sailed for nearly forty years each. They were retired by the Italian Line in the spring of 1965, the same year that the company added the new *Michelangelo* and *Raffaello*. In something of a fleet reshuffling, the *Cristoforo Colombo* became the replacement for the two older ships on the Adriatic route out of Trieste and Venice. Moored together for a time at Trieste, the ships were offered for sale. The *Saturnia* was sold to Italian shipbreakers in October and was broken up at La Spezia, just south of Genoa. The *Vulcania* was sold for further service to another Italian shipping company, the Siosa Lines. She resumed sailing as the *Caribia*, shown here on her maiden voyage in February 1966 (*opposite*). She ran on the England–Spain–West Indies service for a time, then was shifted to weekly seven-day cruises out of Genoa to Cannes, Barcelona, Palma, Bizerta, Palermo, and Naples. The minimum tourist-class fare in the early '70s was just over $100; Dormitory space went for $84. In September 1972, during windy conditions off Cannes, she was driven ashore onto a reef and badly damaged. Too old for major repairs, she was patched up at Genoa, then sold to Italian scrappers at La Spezia. They in turn sold her to breakers at Barcelona, who resold her to Taiwanese scrap merchants, who had her towed out to the Far East. In July 1974, while awaiting a berth at Kaohsiung, the old ship sprang some leaks and began flooding. She was eventually pumped out and then brought into port to finally meet the demolition crews.

After being seized by U.S. authorities at Balboa in the Panama Canal Zone in December 1941, the *Conte Biancamano* was subsequently put to use for the Allied cause. Stripped of her ornate interiors and other passenger ship finery, she was transferred to the U.S. Navy and outfitted as the troopship USS *Hermitage* (*above*). Her first military voyage was a trip from Norfolk to Brisbane, then to Port Suez. With a troop capacity listed as 6,107, she was kept in Pacific waters until May 1944. Thereafter, the *Hermitage* trooped on the Atlantic—to Liverpool, Le Havre, Southampton, and Marseilles. She went back to the Pacific in 1946, and her voyages included visits to Guam and occupied Japan. She is shown here, still in her military livery, on June 27, 1947, at the Bethlehem Steel shipyard in San Francisco Bay. Two months later she was officially returned to the Italian government.

Rebirth and Restoration

About $1 million was spent on the restoration of the *Conte Biancamano* at the Cantieri Riuniti dell'Adriatico shipyard at Monfalcone. Shown (*above*) in the summer of 1948, the ship spent another year being refitted before reentering Italian Line passenger service in November 1949. Her tonnage was altered to 23,562, the overall length to 665 feet, and the accommodations to a more moderate postwar arrangement of 215 in first class, 333 in cabin class, and 1,030 in tourist class.

The *Conte Grande*, was sold to the Americans in April 1942, after having been seized by the Brazilian government eight months earlier. She was refitted as the trooper USS *Monticello* with a wartime capacity listed as 6,890 (as compared to her prewar passenger capacity of 1,718). She traveled in Pacific as well as in Atlantic waters. In 1945, she made a number of Atlantic crossings—to Le Havre or Southampton, with one voyage to Naples in October. She was decommissioned in March 1946 and was laid up for some fifteen months before being returned to the Italians in July 1947.

She reverted to her original name and then underwent an even more strenuous refit and rebuilding than her near-sister, the *Conte Biancamano*. Her interiors were thoroughly restyled and modernized, while the external changes included a reshaped bow and two new wider funnels. She was remeasured at 23,842 gross tons and 667 feet in length. The *Conte Grande* is seen (*opposite, top*) departing from Genoa after a two-year refurbishment on July 14, 1949. She is bound for the east coast of South America—to Rio, Santos, Montevideo, and Buenos Aires.

Beginning in March 1950 and continuing to the very end of her days in 1960, the *Conte Biancamano* divided her services from Genoa: winters to the east coast of South America, summers to Halifax, Nova Scotia (westbound only), and New York. At first assisting the veteran *Saturnia* and *Vulcania*, she was, after her late-1940s refit, the most modern Italian liner on the North Atlantic. Her near-sister, the *Conte Grande*, was just as up to date, as seen by her first-class ballroom and adjoining gallery (*opposite, bottom*).

66 *Rebirth and Restoration*

Rebirth and Restoration 67

68 *Rebirth and Restoration*

The *Conte Grande* had the novelty of having her first-class swimming pool placed between her twin funnels *(opposite)*. Clearly a popular spot during their mild, mid-Atlantic voyages, the cabin-class pool aboard the *Conte Biancamano* *(above)* is seen during the traditional Crossing-of-the-Equator ceremonies held en route to South America. King Neptune and his court are at the far end.

Rebirth and Restoration 69

During her westbound crossings from the Mediterranean to Halifax and New York, the *Conte Biancamano* sometimes encountered heavy weather. As seen from her bridge *(left)*, the ship met with waves as high as 80 feet.

While the *Conte Biancamano* was laid up at Naples in April 1960 and then handed over to the scrappers at La Spezia in the following August, the *Conte Grande*, shown here at Genoa *(below)* with the *Augustus* on the left and the *Cristoforo Colombo* on the right, was chartered to another member of the Finmare Group, Lloyd Triestino, for an immigrant voyage out to Australia. She passed through the Suez Canal, on a routing reminiscent of her prewar Far East voyages, and then sailed onward to Melbourne and Sydney. But then she too went to the La Spezia breakers, on September 7, 1961.

70 *Rebirth and Restoration*

Antoniotto Usodimare

Just as Italy entered the Second World War in 1940, the Italian Line ordered six large cargo ships for its South American services. Three were launched in 1942, the others in 1945. After the war, they were redesigned with more pressing passenger needs in mind and were fitted with quarters for 90 cabin-class passengers and as many as 530 in third class. They were completed in a two-year period, between 1947 and 1949, as the *Paolo Toscanelli*, *Ugolino Vivaldi*, *Sebastiano Caboto*, *Marco Polo*, *Amerigo Vespucci*, and *Antoniotto Usodimare* (**above**), shown departing from Genoa on her maiden voyage). Known as the "Navigatori Class," these six ships sailed from Genoa at three- and four-week intervals. They were then routed to Naples, Cannes, Barcelona, Tenerife, across the mid-Atlantic to La Guaira in Venezuela, Curaçao, Cartagena (Colombia), then through the Panama Canal to Buenaventura (Colombia), Puna (Ecuador), Callao (Peru), and Arica, Antofagasta, and Valparaiso (Chile). The full passage from Genoa to Valparaiso took thirty days. [Built by Ansaldo Shipyard, Genoa, Italy, 1942–49. 9,715 gross tons; 485 feet long; 62 feet wide. Fiat diesel, single screw. Service speed 15 knots. 620 passengers (90 cabin class, 530 third class).]

Cabin class offered a pleasant range of public rooms, such as the veranda as seen aboard the *Sebastiano Caboto* in 1951 (**above**), as well as an outdoor pool, a cinema, and partial air-conditioning. Most of the cabins had private bathroom facilities as well.

All these ships had six cargo holds each, and the third-class dining room, as seen aboard the *Amerigo Vespucci* (**opposite, top**), was built around one of these holds. The tables and benches were collapsible, and the entire area could be used for cargo on the return voyages to Italy.

In later years, in third class, some of the larger dormitories on D Deck, such as those on board the *Amerigo Vespucci* (**opposite, bottom**), were replaced by smaller six- and eight-berth cabins. Overall, this reduced the third-class capacity by approximately 100 berths. In 1958, the *Paolo Toscanelli*, *Sebastiano Caboto*, and *Ugolino Vivaldi* were downgraded to twelve-passenger freighters; the *Amerigo Vespucci*, *Antoniotto Usodimare*, and *Marco Polo* followed in 1963. Mostly, they went into freighter service for Lloyd Triestino. Eventually, they all went to the breakers, the last being scrapped in 1978.

72   *Rebirth and Restoration*

Rebirth and Restoration 73

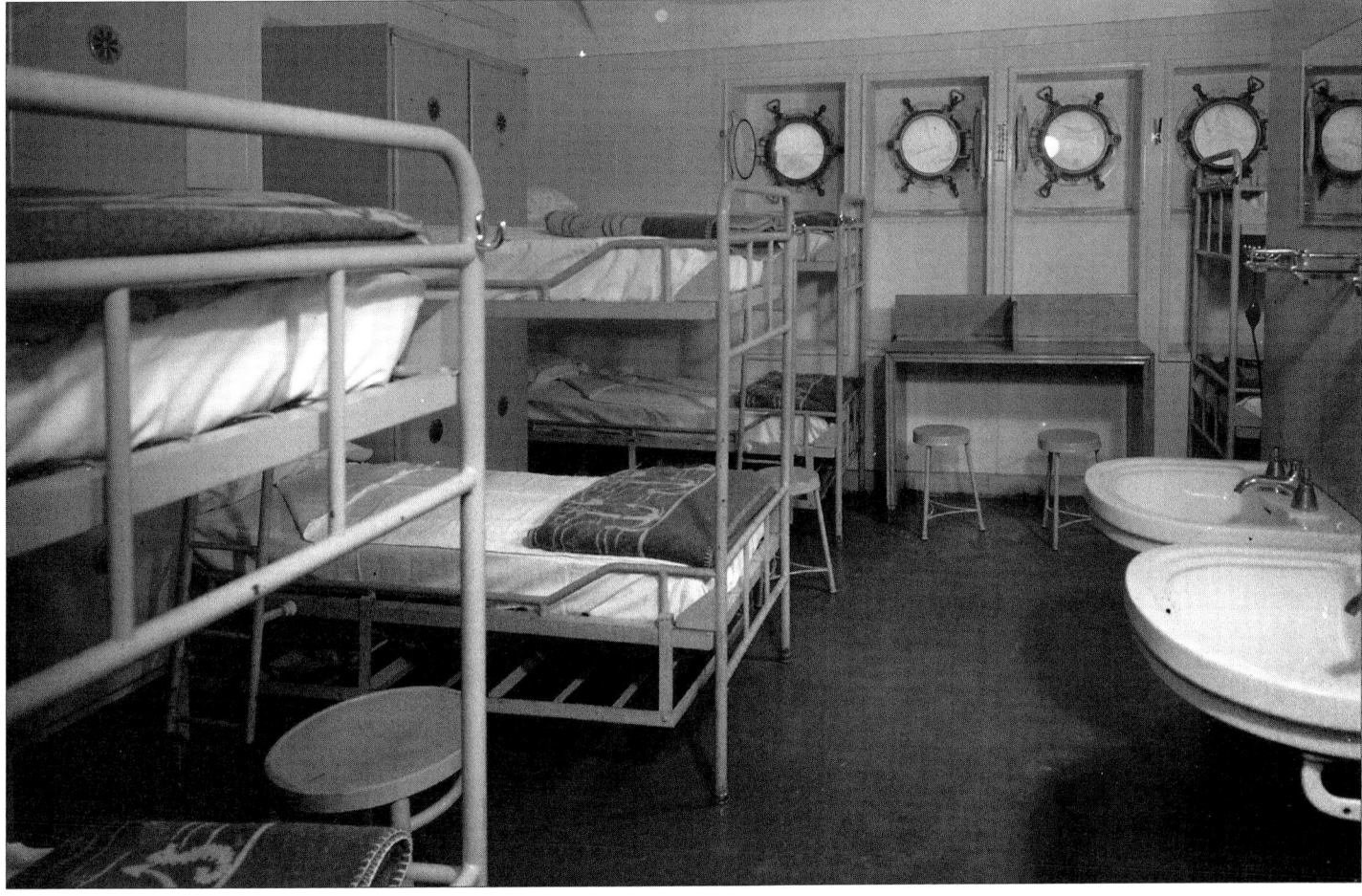

~7~
South American Sisters

"The *Augustus* was my first ship with the great Italian Line. The year was 1960. Service with big luxury liners between Europe and the United States and also between Europe and the east coast of South America was still booming. We carried three classes of passengers [178 in first class, 288 in cabin class and 714 in tourist], and we were always full-up," recalled Captain Nicola Arena. Today, that same 27,000-ton liner lives on, the last of the old Italian Line fleet, but in Far Eastern waters. Now, she's called *Asian Princess*. Actually, she's had a string of other names since her Italian days: *Great Sea, Ocean King, Philippines,* and *President*. Laid up for most of the past two decades, she has moved from anchorage to anchorage, at ports such as Hong Kong, Manila, Subic Bay (also in the Philippines), and Kaohsiung (on Taiwan). Currently, the 680-foot long liner is again rumored—for about the twenty-fifth time—to be headed for a refit and use in Pacific Ocean cruising.

The 21-knot *Augustus* and her twin sister, the *Giulio Cesare* (scrapped in 1973), were designed just after the Second World War in an otherwise ravaged Italy. Marshall Plan monies contributed to their construction, and sets of Fiat diesels, actually built in the late thirties and then warehoused, were used for power. Constructed near Trieste, these twin sisters were completed in 1951–52. Although later used on the North Atlantic run to New York, they were primarily for the South American trade—from Naples, Genoa, Cannes, Barcelona, and Lisbon across the mid-Atlantic to Rio de Janeiro, Santos, Montevideo, and Buenos Aires.

"We had very wealthy passengers in first class, mostly Europeans but also South Americans," recalled Captain Arena. "We'd carry very rich Argentineans and Brazilians, notably the owners of the *estancias*, the big ranches. Usually, they would spend the South American winters, from June through August, in Europe. They'd bring their own servants, cars, even their own horses. From the European end, I remember the Duchess D'Arenberg, who traveled with us each year from Cannes to her other home at Punta del Este. She used to board the ship with the local chief of police, who personally guarded the seven boxes of jewelry that were filled with diamonds and rubies. These were placed immediately in the safe on board the *Augustus*. You don't see that type of passenger any longer. Today, on cruise ships, passengers are far less conspicuous—they no longer exhibit such jewelry. We also carried the Roman Catholic cardinals and their entourages, especially for the papal elections. We also had the ambassadors and, as a courtesy, always flew their national flags. Sometimes, with several on board at once, we would be flying five or six flags. We'd look like the front entrance of the Waldorf-Astoria Hotel in New York!

"In cabin class, we'd have the professional people—the doctors, lawyers, engineers," recalled Arena. "Tourist class was full with immigrants going mostly to Brazil and Argentina, but also some to Chile. These were Italians mostly, but also the Spanish and the Portuguese. We actually had higher quality immigrants going to South America than those on the northern run to New York and to Halifax [where Italian liners also called on their westbound crossings]. On the return trips to Europe, we'd have the young sons and daughters of the earlier immigrants. A trip to Europe was a common graduation present in South American families. In tourist class, we also had the nuns and the priests, the professors and teachers, who were going to Italy for further schooling or for research."

The South American liner trade began to decline in the early '70s. The airlines proved unbeatable rivals. While the *Giulio Cesare* went to the scrappers, the *Augustus* endured a little longer for the Italians, making her last trip in January 1976 before being laid up at Naples. Soon afterward, she was sold to a succession of Eastern owners, most notably the Philippine President Lines, owners of a huge cargo fleet. It will be interesting to see if she sails again.

Giulio Cesare (1951)

Built with Marshall Plan monies, the *Giulio Cesare* (**above**), about to be launched on May 24, 1950, and her twin sister, the *Augustus*, were the first big Italian liners to be built after the war. They were also the beginning of the "new" Italian Line fleet, which would include some of the finest-looking, most luxuriously appointed ships of the 1950s and '60s. Fitted with powerful Fiat diesel engines, which actually dated from 1939, these two new ships ranked among the largest motor liners afloat at the time of their introduction. [Built by Cantieri Riuniti dell'Adriatico, Monfalcone, Italy, 1951. 27,078 gross tons; 681 feet long; 87 feet wide. Fiat diesels, twin screw. Service speed 21 knots. 1,180 passengers (178 first class, 288 cabin class, 714 tourist class).]

The *Giulio Cesare* was a subject of great interest in Italy during the early 1950s. She was a symbol of rebirth, the resurrection of the nation's passenger ship fleet. She is seen here at Trieste *(below)*, about to sail on her first voyage. Afterward, on October 27, 1951, she departed from Genoa on her first voyage to Rio de Janeiro, Santos, Montevideo, and Buenos Aires.

Completely air-conditioned and with such amenities as a swimming pool and an umbrella-lined lido deck for each class, the *Giulio Cesare* and the *Augustus* were noted for their fine contemporary interiors as well. In these two views, we see the first-class ballroom *(opposite, top)* and the main lounge *(opposite, bottom)* aboard the *Giulio Cesare*.

South American Sisters 77

Augustus (1952)

The *Augustus*, shown about to sail from Genoa (***above***), with the *Giulio Cesare* off to the far right, sailed on her maiden voyage to South America in March 1952. [Built by Cantieri Riuniti dell'Adriatico, Trieste, Italy, 1952. 27,090 gross tons; 680 feet long; 87 feet wide. Fiat diesels, twin screw. Service speed 21 knots. 1,180 passengers (178 first class, 288 cabin class, 714 tourist class).]

The *Augustus* was equally as splendid on the inside. These views show the first-class main lounge (***opposite, top***) and the first-class observation lounge (***opposite, middle***). In later years, during a refit, the former first-class ballrooms, like the one shown here aboard the *Augustus* (***opposite, bottom***), were converted to a cinema that included a stage.

79

All of the first-class cabins aboard the *Giulio Cesare* and the *Augustus*, including this twin-bedded room *(above)*, had private bathroom facilities as well as individual telephones. All of the cabin-class rooms, such as this four-berth accommodation, had private shower and toilet facilities *(below)*.

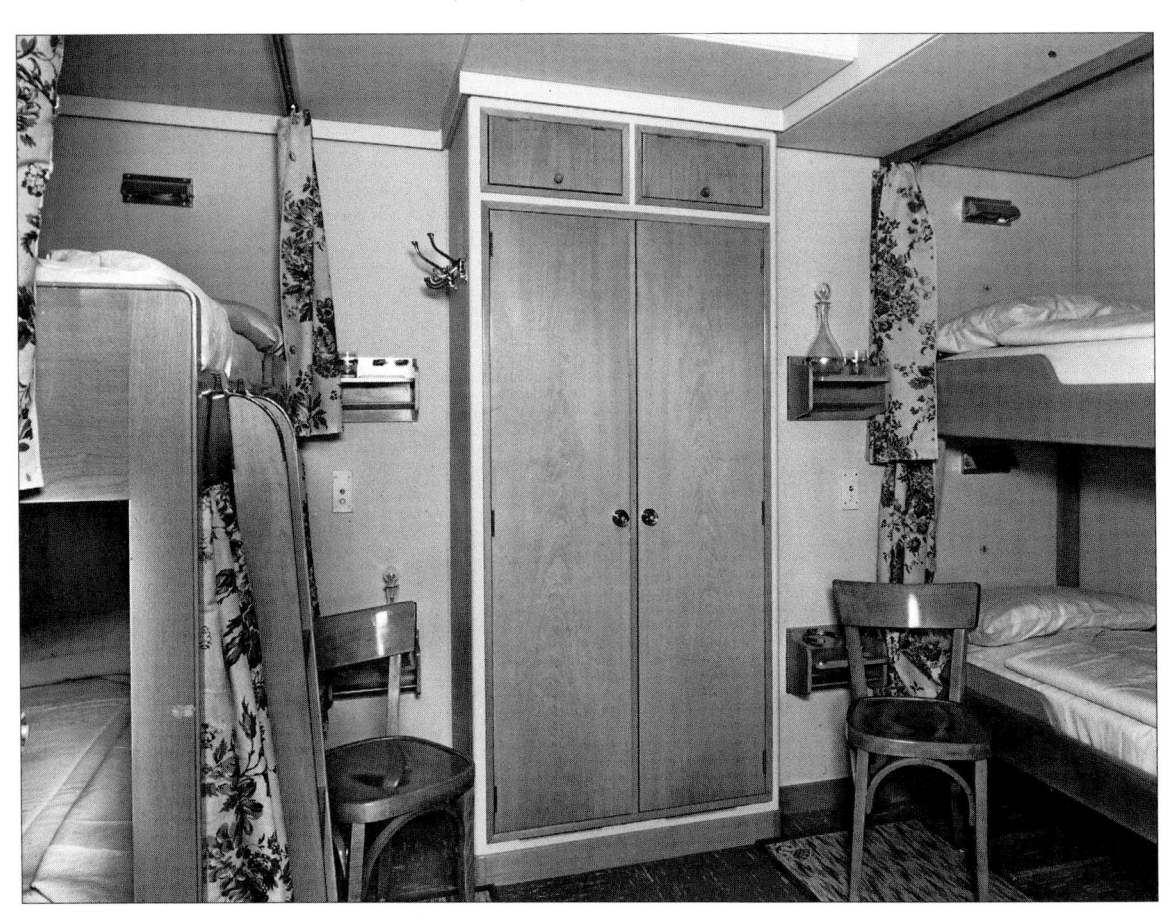

80   *South American Sisters*

In that great tradition of Italian Line ships passing at sea, the eastbound *Giulio Cesare* is given a whistle salute by the South America-bound *Conte Grande* (*above*). The *Giulio Cesare* began to make periodic sailings on the North Atlantic, to New York, in June 1956, joining the *Andrea Doria*, the *Cristoforo Colombo*, the *Conte Biancamano*, the *Saturnia*, and the *Vulcania*. Despite increasing competition from the airlines, the Mediterranean tourist and westbound migrant trades were booming. After the *Andrea Doria* sank, there was a serious gap in the company's schedules. The *Conte Grande* was temporarily reassigned to the New York run as a replacement, and the *Augustus* was brought onto the North Atlantic beginning in February 1957. However, once the brand-new *Leonardo da Vinci* was delivered in the summer of 1960, both of the older liners resumed their South American sailings on a year-round basis. In 1964, they were converted to two-class ships—retaining their original first-class quarters but combining the cabin- and tourist-class sections into one all-tourist class. Each ship now carried 1,000 passengers in revamped tourist-class section.

South American Sisters 81

The *Giulio Cesare* (**above**) developed serious rudder problems during a South American voyage in December 1972. Little effort was made to repair the twenty-year-old, money-losing ship. The South American liner run was in its twilight. Laid up for a time, she was sold to scrappers at La Spezia in the following spring. She is shown in May 1973, awaiting the demolition crews.

The *Augustus* served a while longer than the *Giulio Cesare*, then was laid up at Naples in January 1976. She was sold to Far Eastern interests and sailed under Seychelles, then Panamanian, and finally Philippine registry. Renamed *Great Sea* in 1976 (**below**) and then, after 1980, *Ocean King*, *Philippines*, and *President*, she took her most recent name, *Asian Princess*, in 1987. Since 1976, her only voyages have been moving from anchorage to anchorage, mostly recently in Philippine waters. The last of the Italian Line fleet, the *Augustus* has never returned to passenger service, despite rumors of her revival as a Pacific cruise ship.

82 *South American Sisters*

~8~
Other Italians, Other Routes

When we think of the great Italian Line, we tend to remember its North Atlantic service to New York and such luxury ships as the *Vulcania, Cristoforo Colombo, Leonardo da Vinci,* and the big sisters *Michelangelo* and *Raffaello.* And, of course, the *Andrea Doria* remains welded in memory because of her disastrous sinking off Nantucket in July 1956. But Italian Line also ran passenger ship services to South America—direct to the east coast and then on a separate route via the Panama Canal to ports along the Pacific coast. That latter route is possibly the least known, the least remembered.

After using several smaller, passenger-cargo ships on this run, the Italian Line acquired three fine passenger liners in 1963. They were 12,800-ton sister ships *Australia, Neptunia,* and *Oceania,* all purchased from Lloyd Triestino. The trio had served on the Italy–Australia run since they were built in 1951. After some refitting and the rearrangement of their passenger quarters (to 136 in first class and 536 in tourist), they were rechristened *Donizetti, Rossini,* and *Verdi,* respectively. Quickly, they were dubbed the "Three Musicians."

The 528-foot-long ships offered monthly sailings from Italy. The exact routing was Genoa, Naples, Cannes, and Barcelona, a quick stop at Tenerife in the Canary Islands, and then on to La Guaira, Curaçao, Cartagena, Cristobal, the Panama Canal, Buenaventura, Puna, Callao, Arica, Antofagasta, and finally a turnaround at Valparaiso. Fares for the month-long voyage from Genoa to Valparaiso were set in the early '60s at $600 in first class and $380 in tourist.

"They were very, very good sea vessels," recalled Captain Raffaele Gavino, master of both the *Rossini* and the *Verdi.* "They were easy to handle and responded well. Going out, we still had some Italian and Spanish immigrants by the early 1970s, but mostly it was general passenger traffic by then. I remember that we had lots of French passengers. The immigrants tended to disembark at La Guaira in Venezuela. For cargo, going out, we carried mostly manufactured goods and also lots of religious books and printed matter from Spain. Homeward, we carried copper, coffee, and cocoa. We also brought fruits from Chile and Ecuador up to La Guaira. We also loaded a rather curious cargo at a little island off Ecuador. They were little seeds that are used to make buttons. These went all the way back to Italy."

In the face of the inevitable airline competition, new containerized methods of handling cargo, and soaring Italian-flag operational costs, the Italian Line decided in 1974–75 to end all of its passenger services. The New York run closed altogether in the summer of 1976, as did the run to the west coast of South America. The three sisters were withdrawn and soon sold to Italian shipbreakers at La Spezia. No longer could passengers sail on ships listed as "Valparaiso Bound."

Australia

Trieste-based Lloyd Triestino was the second mightiest Italian passenger ship line, following the Italian Line itself. Both belonged to the government-controlled Finmare Group. Started in 1837, Lloyd Triestino is said to be the oldest active shipping company in the world. A close second, Cunard, was formed three years later. In the early 1950s Lloyd Triestino built three sets of passenger sister ships to replace their wartime losses. The first of these — the *Australia* (**above**) being launched at Trieste on May 21, 1950), the *Neptunia*, and the *Oceania* — were aimed at the Australian market. The launching itself was a significant event. Just before the war, in 1939, the Cantieri Riuniti dell'Adriatico shipyard built seventy-five ships with a total of 620,000 gross tons. After the war, by the early fifties, they had built only four ships with total tonnage of less than 12,000. The Marshall Plan contributed toward the construction of these three liners as well as toward others, providing employment and economic recovery to the area in and around Trieste. [Built by Cantieri Riuniti dell'Adriatico, Trieste, Italy, 1951. 13,140 gross tons; 528 feet long; 69 feet wide. Sulzer diesels, twin screw. Service speed 18 knots. 672 passengers (136 first class, 304 tourist class, 232 third class).]

84 Other Italians, Other Routes

Neptunia

The *Australia*, *Neptunia*, and *Oceania* sailed at mostly monthly intervals from Genoa, Naples, and Messina to Port Said, Suez, Aden, Colombo, and Djakarta, then on to Fremantle, Melbourne, and Sydney, Australia. In this view *(below)*, dated October 11, 1951, the *Neptunia* is arriving at Melbourne for the first time. [Built by Cantieri Riuniti dell'Adriatico, Trieste, Italy, 1951. 13,140 gross tons; 528 feet long; 69 feet wide. Sulzer diesels, twin screw. Service speed 18 knots. 672 passengers (136 first class, 304 tourist class, 232 third class).]

Other Italians, Other Routes

86   *Other Italians, Other Routes*

These new Lloyd Triestino liners were not only modern on the outside but were also decorated in contemporary stylings within. The first-class entrance hall on board the *Australia* (**opposite, top**), is certainly an imposing space. These ships on their outward trips to Australia catered to business people in first class and mostly immigrants in tourist and third class. Two near-sister ships, the *Africa* and the *Europa*, were built especially for the Italy–East and South Africa service. The final pair, the *Asia* and the *Victoria*, ran to the Far East.

In 1963, in something of a reshuffling and an "internal swap" within the Finmare Group, Lloyd Triestino's *Australia*, *Neptunia*, and *Oceania* were transferred over to the Italian Line. They became the so-called "Three Musicians"—the *Donizetti* (**opposite, bottom**), the *Rossini*, and the *Verdi*, respectively. All had been refitted to carry 136 in first class and 536 in tourist. They sailed from Genoa, Cannes, Barcelona, and Lisbon to La Guaira, Curaçao, Cartagena, and Cristobal in the Caribbean, and then, after passing through the Panama Canal, they called along the west coast of South America at Buenaventura, Guayaquil, Callao, Arica, and Valparaiso. The minimum fare in a first-class stateroom for the thirty-day voyage from Genoa all the way to Valparaiso was $600. These ships also carried a considerable amount of cargo—usually general manufactured goods going outward to South America, and returning with the likes of cotton, metals, and sometimes large consignments of coffee. Retired in 1976, the "Three Musicians" went to the breakers at La Spezia. It was the end of Italian Line's passenger service to the west coast of South America.

Victoria (1953)

Finmare had plans in the early 1970s to convert at least some of these Lloyd Triestino liners into all-first-class cruise ships. This changeover never materialized, however. In the end, only the *Victoria*, formerly on the Italy–Far East run, survived. She was transferred in the late summer of 1974 to another Finmare Group member, the Adriatica Line, and used for internal Mediterranean services as well as for occasional cruises. She remained in these services until laid up in June 1977. A year or so later, she was sold to the Youth-With-A-Mission Group. Renamed *Anastasis* (**above**), she has been a roving, worldwide missionary ship ever since. In 1997, she was further refitted so as to maintain her in service until at least 2004. Still a classic-looking vessel, with most of her original design in tact, she is in fact the last survivor of the postwar passenger ships built for Lloyd Triestino. [Built by Cantieri Riuniti dell'Adriatico, Monfalcone, Italy, 1953. 11,693 gross tons; 522 feet long; 68 feet wide. Fiat diesels, twin screw. Service speed 19½ knots. 431 passengers as built (290 first class, 141 tourist class).]

Other Italians, Other Routes 87

Galileo Galilei and Guglielmo Marconi

In the 1960s, Italian shipyards produced some of the world's most notable and best-designed passenger ships. Among these was the *Leonardo da Vinci*, the sisters *Michelangelo* and *Raffaello*, the *Oceanic* and the *Eugenio C*. There were also two very fine liners for Lloyd Triestino, the *Galileo Galilei* and the *Guglielmo Marconi* **(above)** Delivered in April and November of 1963, they provided modern accommodations for as many as 1,700 passengers. Designed with great similarities to the brilliant *Leonardo da Vinci* (1960), these ships were fast (over 27 knots) and brought very high standards to the otherwise budget-priced migrant-oriented Australian market. They could make the passage from Genoa to Sydney in just over twenty-one days. [Built by Cantieri Riuniti dell'Adriatico, Monfalcone, Italy, 1963. 27,900 gross tons; 702 feet long; 94 feet wide. Steam turbines, twin screw. Service speed 24 knots. 1,750 passengers (156 first class, 1,594 tourist class).]

The entrance hall aboard the *Galileo Galilei* (**top**) was typical of Italian modern design in the 1960s: highly polished linoleum flooring, contemporary art on the walls, and overhead fluorescent lighting.

Even into the early 1970s, Australia represented "new life" for many Europeans—Italians as well as Yugoslavs, Greeks, Turks, and even Lebanese. Consequently, these Lloyd Triestino liners were often quite full on their outward sailings to Fremantle, Melbourne, and Sydney. Aboard the *Guglielmo Marconi*, services in the tourist-class restaurant (**middle**) sometimes ran to three sittings, with one being especially for the 200–300 children who might be aboard. The classes shared the shipboard theater (**bottom**)—the upper level was used by the first-class passengers, the lower level by the tourist class.

Other Italians, Other Routes 89

The *Galileo Galilei* and the *Guglielmo Marconi* were the last passenger liners built for Lloyd Triestino. By the early seventies, the airlines had made such inroads in passenger traffic that these liners often sailed less than half full. They were often rerouted on their homeward trips through the South Pacific and the Panama Canal and across the Caribbean and Atlantic to Europe so as to make a complete, possibly more passenger-appealing, round-the-world voyage. In the end, in 1976, the *Marconi* was loaned to the Italian Line to run to the east coast of South America as a companion to another struggling liner, the *Cristoforo Colombo*. In the late 1970s, both ships did some cruising. In December 1978, after an all-too-brief refit and upgrading from her old Australian days, the *Marconi* (**above**) arrived at New York for the first time in hopes of restarting the Italian Line, then known as Italian Line Cruises International. But it all soon failed. In November 1983, both ships were sold off—the *Galileo Galilei* to a Greek-owned company, Chandris-Fantasy Cruises, who refitted her as the Panamanian-registered *Galileo*. In 1989–90, she was rebuilt and renamed the *Meridian*. The *Guglielmo Marconi* went to the Costa Line, who rebuilt her as the *Costa Riviera*. In the fall of 1997, the *Meridian* was sold to Singapore buyers, Metro Holdings, who rechristened her *Sun Vista*. She burned and then sank off the Malaysian coast in May 1999.

Ausonia

Another member of the Finmare Group was the Venice-based Adriatica Line, Adriatica SpA di Navigazione. Their interests were in the eastern Mediterranean and continued, but with passenger ferries and cargo vessels, until they closed in January 1999. But like the Italian Line and Lloyd Triestino, the Adriatica was devastated by the Second World War. By 1945, most of their forty-two ships no longer existed. They began a rebuilding program in the late forties. Unquestionably the finest of their new ships was the flagship, Ausonia (*opposite, bottom*). She followed the design of the *Andrea Doria* and the *Cristoforo Colombo*. Launched in the summer of 1956 and commissioned in October 1957, she was advertised as "the largest and the fastest liner" operating within the confines of the Mediterranean. She sailed between Trieste, Venice, and Brindisi to Beirut and Alexandria. Fully air-conditioned and fitted with stabilizers, she was highly praised not only for her exterior good looks but also for her fine modern accommodations. In 1977, she became a full-time cruise ship and remained as such until sold to Cypriot-based owners, the Louis Cruise Lines, who now sail her as the *Princesa Ausonia*. [Built by Cantieri Riuniti dell'Adriatico, Monfalcone, Italy, 1957. 11,879 gross tons; 522 feet long; 70 feet wide. Steam turbines, twin screw. Service speed 20 knots. 529 passengers (181 first class, 118 second class, 230 third class).]

Homeric

Among other Italian and Italian-related passenger ship companies was the Home Lines. They began sailing, first to South America and later to New York, just after the war, in 1946. They were actually a combination of Italian, Greek, Swiss, and Swedish interests. They specialized in buying second-hand passenger ships and then refitting them, often with expanded capacities. In 1953, for example, they bought the American liner *Mariposa*, formerly owned by the Matson Lines and used on the California–South Pacific run. She had been idle since the end of the war. Renamed *Homeric*, she was rebuilt in 1953–54 to carry over 1,200 passengers for the North Europe–Eastern Canada run and for winter cruising out of New York to the Caribbean. She is seen (*above*) departing on her first Home Lines' voyage from Trieste in January 1955. [Built by Bethlehem Steel Company, Quincy, Massachusetts, 1931. 24,907 gross tons; 638 feet long; 79 feet wide. Steam turbines, twin screw. Service speed 20 knots. 1,243 passengers (147 first class, 1,096 tourist class).]

Other Italians, Other Routes

Oceanic

Another Home Lines ship, the *Oceanic*, was unquestionably one of Italy's finest postwar liners. Although initially intended for seasonal transatlantic service between Cuxhaven (Hamburg), Le Havre, Southampton, Quebec City, and Montreal, with wintertime tropical cruising from New York, she was assigned to cruise sailings from the start, in April 1965. She was a pioneer of seven-day, Saturday-to-Saturday, year-round, leisure service between New York and Nassau. Her splendid decor and accommodations were matched by such amenities as a retractable glass roof over her midships swimming pools and lido area. She is shown (***above***), on November 26, 1968, while undergoing her annual refit at the Newport News shipyard in Virginia. Behind is the superliner *United States*, the world's fastest passenger ship, which would be decommissioned in November 1969. [Built by Cantieri Riuniti dell'Adriatico, Monfalcone, Italy, 1965. 39,241 gross tons; 774 feet long; 96 feet wide. Steam turbines, twin screw. Service speed 26.5 knots. 1,600 maximum passengers).]

Other Italians, Other Routes

Castel Felice

Another Italian-based company was the Sitmar Line (for Società Italiana Trasporti Marittimi). They specialized in the low-fare tourist and migrant trades. After converting several ex-American vessels, in 1952 they bought the former *Kenya* of the British India Line. She was then rebuilt as the *Castel Felice* and was used on a variety of services: Europe–Australia, Europe–West Indies, Europe–South America, and on the transatlantic run to New York and to eastern Canada. In later years, she was permanently assigned to the Australian route—sailing from Bremerhaven, Rotterdam, Southampton, and Naples to Port Said, Suez, Aden, Fremantle, Melbourne, and Sydney. She is seen *(below)*, on February 2, 1956, making a special call at Valletta on Malta to receive several hundred Maltese migrants bound for new lives in Australia. The Swedish passenger ship *Saga* is to the left, carrying 400 Germans on a charter Mediterranean cruise. The British aircraft carrier HMS *Centaur* is in the background. [Built by Alexander Stephen & Sons Limited, Glasgow, Scotland, 1930. 12,478 gross tons; 493 feet long; 64 feet wide. Steam turbines, twin screw. Service speed 17 knots. 1,540 passengers (596 first class, 944 tourist class).]

Aurelia

The Cogedar Line was another Italian acronym for a long corporate title: Compagnia Genovese d'Armamento. They started carrying migrants in converted freighters in the late forties. One of their best-known ships was the *Aurelia* (**above**), purchased in 1954 for the Europe–Australia and later around-the-world tourist trades. She had been the *Huascaran* on the Hamburg America Line's service to the west coast of South America, then after the war became Canadian Pacific's *Beaverbrae*. She then sailed for Cogedar until 1968 and afterward became the Greek cruise ship *Romanza*. She became the *Romantica* in 1991, but then was a total loss following a fire in the eastern Mediterranean in October 1997. Her remains were later scrapped in Egypt. [Built by Blohm & Voss Shipbuilders, Hamburg, Germany, 1939. 10,480 gross tons; 487 feet long; 60 feet wide. Diesel-electric, single screw. Service speed 17 knots. 1,124 all-tourist class passengers.]

Sydney

Naples-based Flotta Lauro, the Lauro Line, was also engaged in the low-fare and migrant trades. They were also involved in converting older passenger ships as well as surplus wartime tonnage. Having been auxiliary aircraft carriers, the *Sydney* (**below**), shown at Valletta, Malta, on May 24, 1957, and her sister ship, the *Roma*, were strikingly rebuilt as passenger ships by Lauro in 1949–51. They too were used on the very busy, postwar Australian trade. They were, in their time, considered to be two of the finest migrant ships afloat. They had modern Italian decor, fine cuisine, outdoor swimming pools, and even open-air cinemas. [Built by Western Pipe & Steel Company, San Francisco, California, 1944. 14,687 gross tons; 492 feet long; 69 feet wide. Steam turbines, single screw. Service speed 17 knots. 1,113 passengers (119 first class, 994 tourist class).]

Other Italians, Other Routes

On the South American route, to Rio, Santos, Montevideo, and Buenos Aires, the greatest competitor to the Italian Line passenger ships was the Costa Line. Genoa-based as well, they amassed a fine fleet soon after the Second World War. They were noted for having some of the best interior design of any ships under the Italian flag. Later, they turned to cruising and, by the early 1980s, had the largest cruise fleet in the Western world (only the Soviets had a bigger one). In this busy scene at Genoa, three Costa liners were in port together *(above)*: With large C's on their funnels, from right to left, they are the flagship *Federico C.*, the *Anna C.*, and the *Bianca C.* Also in this group is the Spanish-flag *Cabo San Vicente* of the Ybarra Line, with the double-X on its funnel.

96 *Other Italians, Other Routes*

Eugenio C.

The 1960s were a highly productive era for Italian shipyards. Among launchings were the *Leonardo da Vinci*, the *Galileo Galilei* and *Guglielmo Marconi*, the *Michelangelo* and *Raffaello*, and the *Oceanic*. Another superb ship was Costa's new flagship, *Eugenio C.* (*above*). She was the largest, fastest, and most luxurious liner of her day on the Italy–South America run. She was also the last to be built for that dwindling three-class service. She became the British-owned *Edinburgh Castle* in 1997, refitted to run cruises from New York and later British ports. By late 1998, however, she was laid up, bankrupt and for sale. [Built by Cantieri Riuniti dell'Adriatico, Monfalcone, Italy, 1966. 30,567 gross tons; 712 feet long; 96 feet wide. Steam turbines, twin screw. Service speed 27 knots. 1,636 passengers (178 first class, 356 cabin class, 1,102 tourist class).]

The first-class nightclub (*below*) was done in high standard modern aboard the *Eugenio C.* It was typical of the decor aboard "showcase" Italian-built liners of the period.

~9~
Renaissance Ships

"Every night was a 'Gala Night' in the first class on the Italian Line," remembered Captain Nicola Arena, who started with the company in 1958 and then remained until the very last passenger sailing nearly twenty years later, in 1977. "The activities in first class seemed to start with four-o'clock teatime. There was soft, classical music provided by a twelve-piece orchestra," he recalled. "Later, predinner drinks were in the cocktail lounge. There would be smoked salmon and caviar. Violinists played as a backdrop. It was formal every night, and the women wore different dresses for as many nights at sea. We had celebrities, government officials, and some very rich people. Mostly, they traveled with lots of luggage, twenty bags or more. We had huge luggage rooms on board. They'd also have their automobiles in the hold.

"In the evenings after dinner, there was dancing," added Arena. "We had special social hostesses, who were Italian, German, and Swiss. They came from aristocratic backgrounds themselves, from the great European families. They mixed perfectly with the passengers. I especially remember Baroness Longobardi. She came from one of the great Venetian families and was also a soprano."

Captain Arena, who left the Technical Department and became a senior purser, served on most of the grand Italian Line luxury passenger ships of the 1960s and '70s—the *Conte Biancamano*, the *Cristoforo Colombo*, the *Augustus*, the *Giulio Cesare*, the *Leonardo da Vinci*, and the superliners *Michelangelo* and *Raffaello*. He also sailed the South American run on such ships as the *Marco Polo* and the *Verdi*.

The New York run had been fully restored when, in early 1953, the luxurious, powerful *Andrea Doria* crossed on her maiden voyage to New York's Pier 84. Tugs, fireboats, and overhead helicopters joined in the welcome. She was followed, in the summer of 1954, by a sister ship, the *Cristoforo Colombo*. The untimely sinking of the *Doria* in July 1956 led to immediate plans for a replacement. A larger, improved version of these earlier sisters was commissioned in the summer of 1960 as the *Leonardo da Vinci*. Coming in the wake of earlier, prewar liners such as the *Saturnia*, the *Vulcania*, and the *Conte Biancamano*, these luxury vessels of the fifties were called Italy's "renaissance ships."

"On the New York run to and from Naples, Genoa, Cannes, and Gibraltar, we had many, many famous passengers," added Captain Arena. "There was the king of Morocco, Paul Newman, Elizabeth Taylor, Renata Tebaldi, all the tenors from La Scala, the Duke and Duchess of Windsor, members of the Roosevelt and Rockefeller families, Dustin Hoffman, and Alberto Sordi, the popular Italian comedian. I recall that the king of Morocco took an entire deck on the *Raffaello*. He traveled with an entourage of 137, which included concubines. Desert warriors served as his twenty-four-hour guards and used colorful swords and spears. The Duke and Duchess of Windsor sailed with a secretary, a maid, a butler, and their five pug dogs. Gloria Swanson brought along all of her own health foods and mineral water. We also had many of the Catholic cardinals. Mostly, these celebrity passengers were given the very best cabins. They wanted more privacy, had the best staff to look after them, and often dined in their rooms.

"In cabin class, we had the professionals—the doctors and the lawyers—and sometimes their entire families," noted Arena. "Tourist class to North America was mostly immigrants—usually Italians, but also Yugoslavs, Spaniards, Eastern Europeans, and even Germans. But by the early 1970s, the cost of running these big, expensive liners was too high. The airlines were unbeatable competitors, and so the Italian Line lost money. The government persisted with generous subsidies, but finally conceded in 1975–76. The great days of the Italian Line and their luxury passenger fleet were over. Ships like the *Cristoforo Colombo* were sold to the Venezuelans, and the *Leonardo da Vinci* was laid up. In many ways, we shall never again see ships like them."

Andrea Doria

After the completion of the *Giulio Cesare* and the *Augustus* in 1951–52, the Italian Line turned its attention to a larger, more powerful, even more luxurious pair of sister ships for the demanding American trade. They would be used on the express run, on a year-round schedule in those waning, precruise times. The *Andrea Doria*, which was built using quite advanced prefabrication methods during her construction, is shown (***above***) at the Ansaldo shipyard at Sestri Ponente, near Genoa, in August 1952. She would be commissioned that December. [Built by Ansaldo Shipyards, Genoa, Italy, 1953. 29,093 gross tons; 700 feet long; 90 feet wide. Steam turbines, twin screw. Service speed 23 knots. 1,241 passengers (218 first class, 320 cabin class, 703 tourist class).]

Renaissance Ships

100 Renaissance Ships

The *Andrea Doria*, named for the Genoese naval hero of the early 16th century, left Genoa on her maiden Atlantic crossing on January 14, 1953. She received a gala New York harbor reception *(opposite, top)* and was hailed by the press as a symbol of "the rebirth of the Italian merchant marine." From 1946 until 1953, American Export Lines was the chief U.S. agent for the Italian Line. A display in the street-level windows of Export's headquarters in lower Manhattan, at 39 Broadway, welcomed the brand-new *Andrea Doria* *(opposite, bottom)*. Italian Line later opened their own offices at 24 State Street and then at 1 Whitehall Street.

The Italians were aptly proud of the brand-new *Andrea Doria* and, later, of her sister ship, the *Cristoforo Colombo*. These ships were superbly crafted and handsome inside and out—the perfect rivals to American Export Lines' *Independence* and *Constitution*, which had arrived two years earlier. As national flagship, the *Andrea Doria* received the most attention. Not only was she the biggest vessel in the entire Italian merchant marine (it was long before the era of supertankers), but she was also the fastest, having attained a speed of over 26 knots during her trials in the western Mediterranean. Outbound from New York harbor *(above)*, she was able to cross the Atlantic in six days.

Renaissance Ships 101

102   *Renaissance Ships*

When she was commissioned in 1953, the *Andrea Doria* was one of the most modern liners in the world. The first-class main lounge (*opposite, top*) was a room of style, comfort, and simplicity. Certainly, the *Doria's* interiors were in startling contrast to the richly ornate, visually busy stylings of the prewar Italian liners and, more noticeably, to those of her postwar fleetmates, the *Saturnia* and the *Vulcania*, which still bore their 1920s Italian decor. The first-class public rooms aboard the *Andrea Doria*—as exemplified by the ballroom (*opposite, middle*) and the bar (*opposite, bottom*)—exhibited the Italian flair for tasteful modern interior design. The first-class children's playroom (*above*) was decorated with colorful murals along the walls. In the bedroom of a deluxe cabin (*left*), there were numerous closets and a pull-down writing desk. The indirect ceiling lighting was unique to passenger liners in the 1950s.

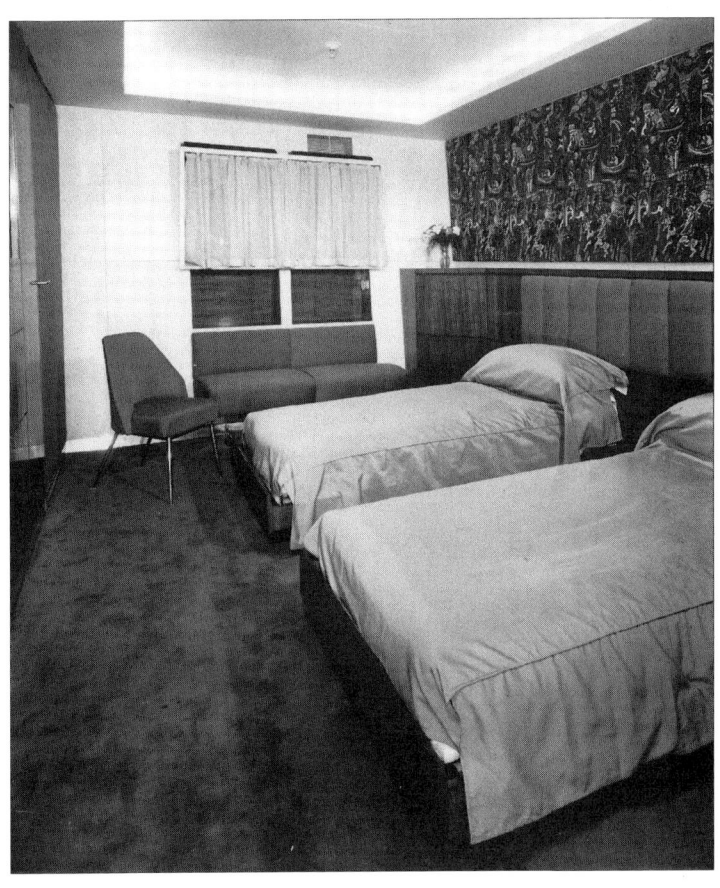

Renaissance Ships 103

The Italian Line ships were often among the great gatherings of vessels along New York's Luxury Liner Row. In this view (*above*), entitled "Seagoing Queens Hold Court" and dated October 26, 1955, five Atlantic liners are shown: From top to to bottom, the *Mauretania* and the *Queen Elizabeth*, Cunard Line; the *Liberté*, French Line; the *United States*, United States Lines; the *Andrea Doria*; and the *Independence*, American Export Lines.

104   Renaissance Ships

The *Andrea Doria* is, of course, best remembered for her fatal collision off the American east coast in the summer of 1956, her fourth year of service. Several books, numerous magazine articles, and some television documentaries have attempted to analyze this disaster. When it occurred, on the night of July 25th, the liner was some sixty miles from Nantucket and just hours from her arrival at New York's Pier 84. In foggy conditions, she was rammed by the outbound Swedish American liner *Stockholm*, which had left Pier 97 that morning. A huge hole was torn in the *Andrea Doria's* side, just below the starboard bridge. The collision caused a sudden and very immediate list, making it impossible for the crew to lower any of the *Doria's* port-side lifeboats. There was time, however, for adequate evacuation because the ship remained afloat for hours. Finally abandoned, she sank in the morning hours of July 26th.

Renaissance Ships 105

The 12,644-ton *Stockholm* limped back to New York, her bow smashed (**left**). She looked forlorn to some, sinister to others, as she slowly made her way up the Lower Bay and along the Hudson. In all, there were fifty-two casualties in the disaster.

The mood at the Italian Line offices, both in Genoa and in New York, was grim. The Italians had lost a flagship, a vessel sometimes said to be so well designed and constructed as to be unsinkable. It was a very deep blow to Italian pride. Long, confidential inquiries and hearings followed the tragedy. The compensation amounted to $48 million, but precise responsibility was never revealed. The final investigations were dropped by the mutual consent of the Italian Line and the Swedish American Line.

The *Andrea Doria* herself, resting on her starboard side in the cold waters of the western Atlantic, has been inspected by many divers. The foyer statue of Andrea Doria along with the ship's safe have been retrieved. In 1982, a lifeboat washed ashore on Staten Island, a few miles from the ship's intended berth in Manhattan.

Cristoforo Colombo

With the *Andrea Doria* gone, her sister ship, the slightly less prestigious *Cristoforo Colombo*, became the national flagship. She was not surpassed until the *Doria*'s replacement arrived, in June 1960. In this view, dated June 1954, the *Cristoforo Colombo* is seen in a photo taken from the *Doria* (**below**). The *Colombo* is preparing to sail on her maiden voyage to New York. [Built by Ansaldo Shipyards, Genoa, Italy, 1954. 29,191 gross tons; 700 feet long; 90 feet wide. Steam turbines, twin screw. Service speed 23 knots. 1,055 passengers (229 first class, 222 cabin class, 604 tourist class).]

The *Cristoforo Colombo* leaves Genoa on her maiden voyage to New York, July 15, 1954 (*above*). Lauro Lines' *Sydney*, a passenger ship on the Italy–Australia run, is to the left.

A gathering at Genoa (*below*): two New York express liners and two South American ships: From left to right, the *Andrea Doria*, the *Giulio Cesare*, the *Conte Grande*, and the *Cristoforo Colombo*.

Renaissance Ships 107

On February 5, 1957, the mighty *Colombo* (***above***) arrived at New York's Pier 84 without the aid of Moran tugboats. Using her own anchor, she cautiously moved toward the pier, moving sideways by alternative use of her engines.

These interior views of the *Cristoforo Colombo* are of her first-class ballroom (***opposite, top***), part of the first-class dining room (***opposite, middle***), and an apartment deluxe (***opposite, bottom***). That suite was priced at $1,000 per person in peak summers for the eight days to Naples or the nine days to Cannes and Genoa from New York.

108 *Renaissance Ships*

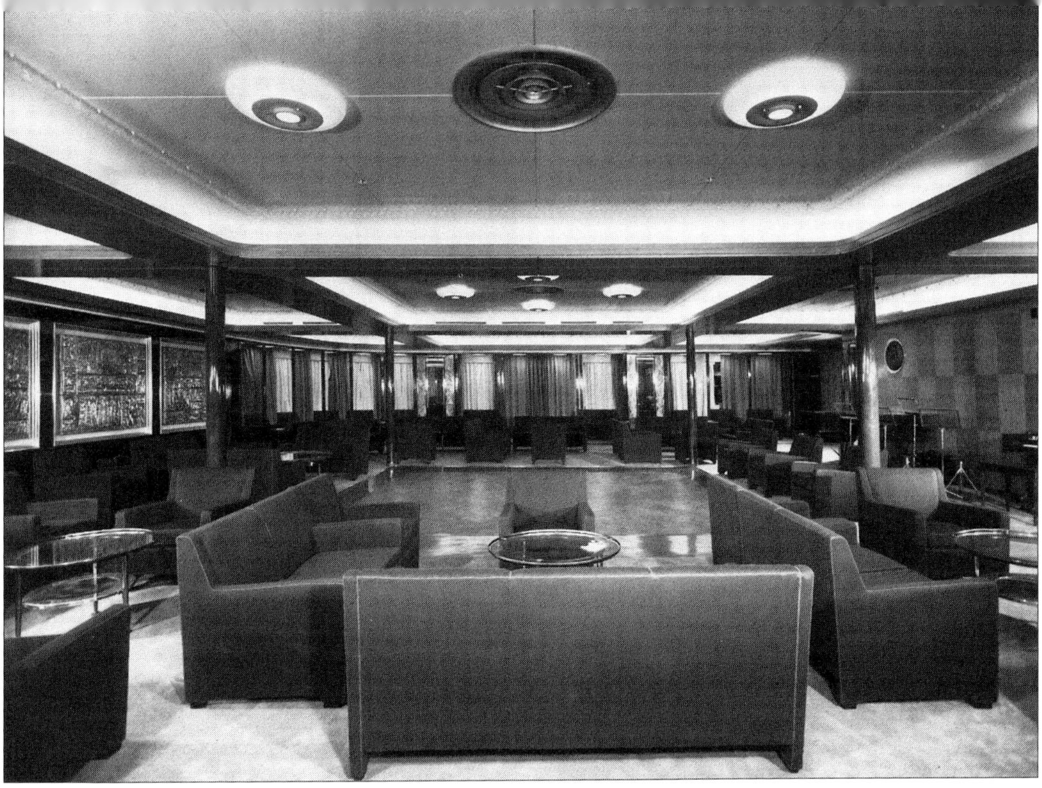

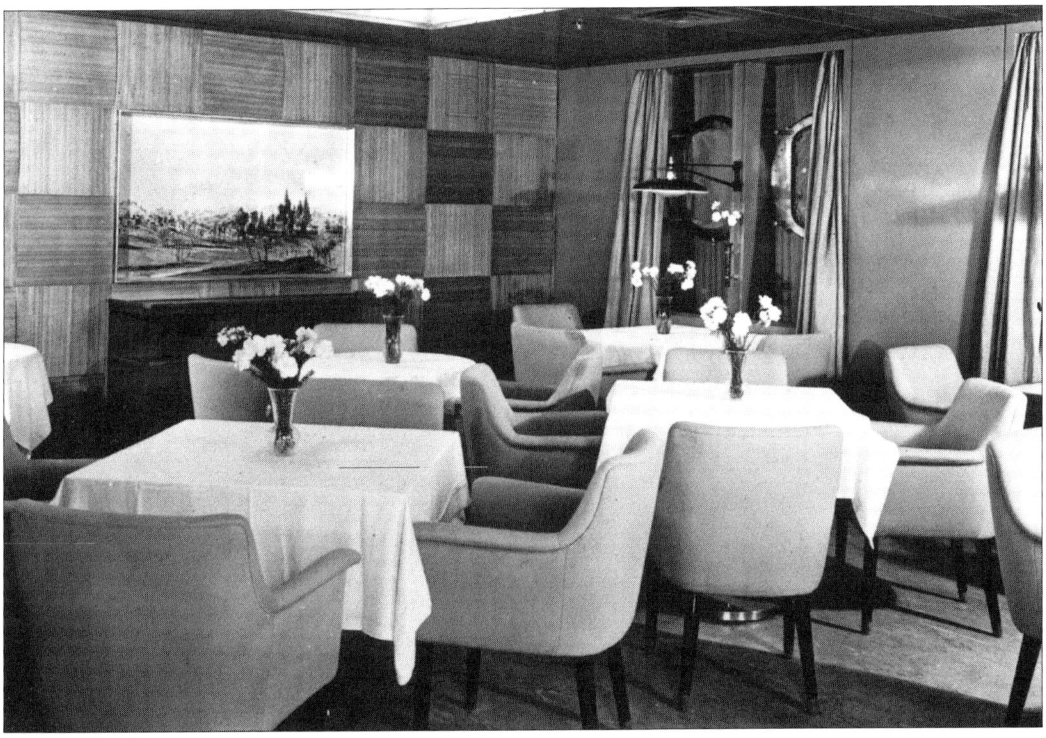

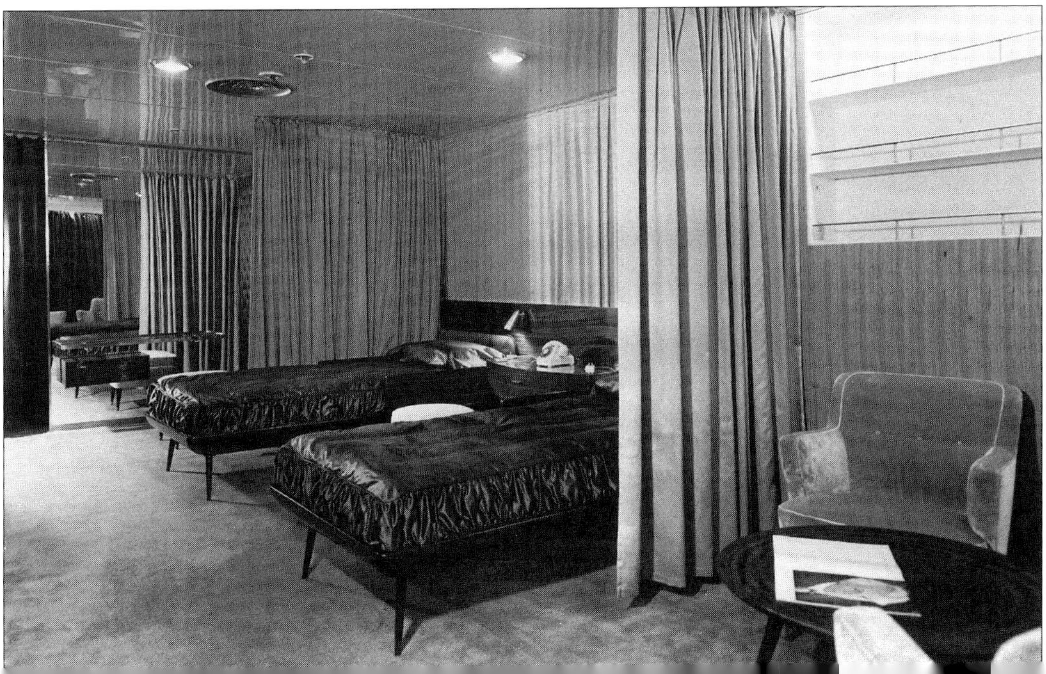

In the spring of 1964, the *Pietà* from the Vatican was carried to New York for the World's Fair aboard the *Cristoforo Colombo*. At Naples, the ship was put specially in dry dock so that she would not move at all during loading process. A big crane maneuvered the case, which was filled with plastic foam. It was lowered onto a rubber base placed in the bottom of the first-class pool. The crate was made to be easily floatable in case of sinking. It was secured only by easily releasable snap hooks. At New York the precious cargo was lifted from the *Colombo* onto a barge alongside by a heavy-lift floating crane (**left**).

The *Colombo* (**below**) remained an express ship on the Naples–Genoa–New York run until the spring of 1965, when the much larger and faster *Michelangelo* and *Raffaello* first arrived. The older ship then replaced the veteran *Saturnia* and *Vulcania* on the Adriatic service. In 1966, the liner was repainted white to match the rest of the Italian Line passenger fleet. The *Colombo* was rather abruptly reassigned to the South American route in February 1973. The *Giulio Cesare* had just been withdrawn because of mechanical troubles, prompting a rearrangement of the fleet. Actually, ships such as the *Colombo* were already largely unprofitable by this time. In 1977, as one of the last government-owned Italian liners, the *Colombo* was withdrawn and sold to Venezuelan interests, who used her as an accommodation ship for workers at Puerto Ordaz. She was resold in 1981 to Taiwanese scrappers, who had her towed across the Pacific to Kaohsiung. The scrappers then decided to resell her and towed her to Hong Kong. There were no buyers, however, and in the fall of 1982 she was returned to Kaohsiung and scrapped.

110 *Renaissance Ships*

Leonardo da Vinci

This ship emerged primarily as a replacement for the ill-fated *Andrea Doria*. In the late 1950s, the Italian Line's Mediterranean–New York passenger trade was still booming, and the sisters *Giulio Cesare* and *Augustus* had to be swung off the South American route to fill the gap left by the *Doria's* demise. A third of Italian Line's management sat through the tedious court proceedings and investigations of the *Doria* disaster. Another third handled the line's normal day-to-day operations, while the final third planned for a new transatlantic liner. She was launched as the *Leonardo da Vinci* by Signora Carla Gronchi, wife of the president of Italy, on December 7, 1958. [Built by Ansaldo Shipyards, Genoa, Italy, 1960. 33,340 gross tons; 761 feet long; 92 feet wide. Steam turbines, twin screw. Service speed 23 knots. 1,326 passengers (413 first class, 342 cabin class, 571 tourist class).]

Renaissance Ships

The plans of the *Giulio Cesare* and the *Augustus* of 1951–52 and of the *Andrea Doria* and the *Cristoforo Colombo* of 1953–54 were reviewed as part of the preparation for construction of the *Leonardo*. The basic design of the new ship was similar but with vast improvements—such as the elimination of the aft cargo space so as to create more lido areas for passengers (including six swimming pools, the first class one of which was heated by infrared rays), the installation of far more private plumbing in the cabins (as much as an 80 percent increase in tourist class), and even a look into the future such that her steam turbine machinery was said to be easily convertible, as early as 1965, to nuclear power. In short, the *Leonardo da Vinci* was the very finest liner Italy could produce at the time. She is shown on a July morning in 1960, arriving in New York for the first time *(above)*. In lower Manhattan, the classic Woolworth Building is at the right, foreground.

The *Leonardo* arrived with an escort of spraying fireboats, tugs, and buzzing helicopters (***above***). The welcoming fetes included gala pierside parties, elegant luncheons, and even an open house for the general public. The Italians were rightfully proud of their new flagship, certain that it would erase the tragic image of the *Andrea Doria*. There were some blemishes, however. The new ship had stability problems, and so some 3,000 tons of iron had to be placed along her double bottom. Therefore, being heavier, she had a much higher fuel consumption than expected. Overall, she became the most expensive liner to operate within the Italian Line fleet.

The interiors, such as this first-class ballroom aboard the *Leonardo da Vinci* (***below***) were more modern, perhaps even better designed and appointed, than those aboard the earlier *Andrea Doria* and *Cristoforo Colombo*. Between 1960 and 1965, until the advent of the sisters *Michelangelo* and *Raffaello*, the *da Vinci* was the finest ship in Mediterranean service.

This dramatic aerial photograph, taken on July 10, 1963, records another great gathering of Atlantic liners along New York's West Side piers. From top to bottom are the *Queen Mary*, Cunard Line; the *France*, French Line; the *Olympia*, Greek Line; the *Atlantic*, American Export Lines; the *Leonardo da Vinci*; and finally, the *Independence*, also American Export.

114 Renaissance Ships

Renaissance Ships 115

The *da Vinci's* black hull took on a more tropical flavor in 1966, when she was repainted in solid white. Cruising had, by the early seventies, become more and more her mainstay, especially as Italian Line's transatlantic traffic slipped into decline. Embarrassing newspaper articles, especially in the Italian press, commented on the large number of unionized crew members serving fewer and fewer passengers. The *da Vinci* alone cost the government $30,000 a day to run, with a subsidy of over $700 for each passenger carried. Shown in this nighttime view at Genoa (**above**), the proud *da Vinci*, like her Italian Line fleetmates, had fallen on hard times.

Shown here sailing from New York on a winter's day (**right**), the *da Vinci* had been berthed between the *Bremen* (left) and the *Cristoforo Colombo* (right). The *da Vinci* was always a popular ship, first teamed with the *Colombo* on the Atlantic express run, then with additional ports of call in the Mediterranean after the larger *Michelangelo* and *Raffaelo* took over most of the transatlantic business after 1965. Among the cities where the *da Vinci* called were Palma, Messina, Palermo, Barcelona, Casablanca, Lisbon, Madeira, and Las Palmas. She also made periodic cruises, mostly in winter, to the Caribbean and South America. A highlight was her annual mid-winter voyage around the entire Mediterranean. This fifty-one-day cruise, which left New York on February 15, 1963, was priced from $1,495. Her most adventurous trip, however, was a forty-one-day cruise in February 1970, when she sailed through the Panama Canal to Hawaii.

116   Renaissance Ships

The *Leonardo da Vinci* closed out the Italian Line transatlantic service in June 1976, then sat idle for a time awaiting reassignment. In July 1977, she was reactivated by the newly formed, union-inspired Italian Line Cruises International for Miami-Nassau overnight cruises. Her managers now were, in fact, other Italians, the Costa Line. Little was actually done to upgrade the ship. In fact, the sparkle was gone. She proved far too big for that service and far too expensive to operate. Her fuel costs were staggering. She was soon back in Italy, laid up at La Spezia. There were rumors of further cruising, possible luxury service out of New York, use as a floating hotel, and even refitting her as a casino ship moored in the River Thames at London. All plans failed to materialize. Sadly, on July 4, 1980, while at anchor, a mysterious fire burned through the great liner for four days. Thousands flocked to the shoreline as smoke filled the skies above. In the end, the charred corpse was towed outside La Spezia's main harbor and left half-submerged in forty feet of water, and with a sixty-degree list *(top)*. The splendid *Leonardo da Vinci* was finished, although still heavily surrounded in controversy. Righted and then brought back into La Spezia to meet the wrecking crews *(middle and bottom)*, she was worth only $1 million in scrap value, much less than the $7.7 million insurance she had carried. Her last remains were gone by 1982.

Renaissance Ships 117

~10~
The Italian Superliners

"They lost money from the very start. They lived off the very generous subsidies given by the Italian government. It was all really a big, lavish dream that these ships would persist and finally succeed," said Captain Nicola Arena. He was recalling the 45,000-ton superliners *Michelangelo* and *Raffaello*, the biggest and grandest Italian ships built in the 1960s. These 1,775-passenger ships were even longer than the prewar *Rex*.

Completed just months apart in 1965, the 902-foot-long *Michelangelo* and *Raffaello* were built at Genoa and at Monfalcone, respectively. They were designed to maintain the old express run to New York—eight days from Naples, seven from Genoa, and five from Gibraltar. First-class fares in 1965 started at $425, while a tourist-class berth cost $275. Splendid in all-white paint, these luxury liners had such amenities as six swimming pools, lavish public rooms, and at least one private shower and toilet in every cabin.

"The first sketches of what would become the *Michelangelo* and the *Raffaello* were actually drawn in 1958," according to Maurizio Eliseo. "They had black hulls, not white. The two funnels did not have lattice work. The lattice style was first intended for the sister ships *Guglielmo Marconi* and *Galileo Galilei* [built 1963]. But their owners, Lloyd Triestino, did not approve, and so they were used instead on the *Michelangelo* and *Raffaello*. These funnels were designed by Professor Mortarino of Turin Polytechnic."

Arriving just three years after the French Line took delivery of their 66,300-ton *France* and four years before Cunard's *Queen Elizabeth 2*, a 65,800-tonner, these Italian twins cost $120 million, a hefty amount for the '60s. They were improved, larger versions of the *Leonardo da Vinci*, which first arrived in 1960. But since the airlines had begun to dominate the transatlantic travel business in 1958–59, the creation of these two large, lavish Italians was misguided at best. In fact, these ships never earned a single lira in profit. Subsidies from Rome ran as high as $700 for every passenger carried. Even attempts at tropical, all-one-class, New York–based cruising failed. Rather incredibly, the new ships continued to sail for a full decade, until 1975.

"The Italian Line directors in those days were not marketing people. They didn't see or recognize trends," added Captain Arena. "It was all quite clear, however. The Atlantic passenger trade was just about finished. But the directors had their own preferences. They wanted big, prestigious ships. They actually tried to defy the trend, the decline of transatlantic passenger shipping. And so, the *Michelangelo* and *Raffaello* were totally uneconomical.

"They were big losers. Often, they carried more crew than fare-paying passengers. And the Italian seamen's unions were no help. They were unbreakable. They were, of course, influenced by the socialist movements in Italy of the late 1960s. They felt that the government would never close the Italian Line. It was all a disaster really—the end was coming. It was too late even for cruising for that type of ship."

With the aged and frail Duchess of Windsor aboard, the *Michelangelo* made the last crossing in July 1975. Soon, stripped of their artworks and other finery, the two big liners were moored at an anchorage south of Genoa, at La Spezia, to await sale. Norwegian Caribbean Lines thought of converting them into Caribbean cruise ships, the Brazilians thought of making them into stationary sites for low-cost housing, and a Lichtenstein-based organization wanted to restyle them as floating cancer research and treatment clinics. "I remember that Captain Mario Vespa, then the chairman of the hugely successful Home Lines, approached Finmare, the government group that owned the two ships, in 1976," added Captain Arena. "He offered a reasonable price, planned to keep the Italian crews, and envisioned them in American cruise services. But the Italian government ministers wouldn't hear of it. The ships were liabilities, the subjects of government misspending and poor press. They wanted to be rid of them. And so, they were sold to the Shah of Iran's government for use as accommodation ships for army personnel, navy trainees, and oil workers."

In 1977, the *Michelangelo* went into "exile" to Bandar Abbas, the *Raffaello* to Bushire, in Iran. But life for the ships was never again the same. Even the liaison crews from Italian Line left, disheartened. The ships fell quickly into disrepair and neglect, and were said to be invaded by small armies of rats. The *Raffaello* was sunk in an Iraqi missile attack in February 1983, and the *Michelangelo* went to nearby Pakistani scrappers in 1991. It was a sad ending for these two magnificent ships.

Michelangelo

The Italians had the proven ability to build glorious ships, but they were less than sensible when they launched not one but two superliners as late as 1965. The airlines were already dominant on the transatlantic run. They had 63 percent of the traffic in 1959 and as much as 95 percent by 1965. In ten years of service, neither the *Michelangelo* (*above*) nor the *Raffaello* earned a profit. They were sometimes known in Italy as the "make-work ships"—to provide jobs for shipyard workers, dockers, and the crew members. As the *Michelangelo* was fitting out at Genoa (*below*), press releases described her alluring details: six outdoor pools (three for adults, three for children), private bathroom facilities in every cabin (even in the least expensive four-berth room), and a faster sailing time across the Mediterranean and Atlantic.[Built by Ansaldo Shipyards, Genoa, Italy, 1965. 45,911 gross tons; 902 feet long; 102 feet wide. Steam turbines, twin screw. Service speed 26.5 knots. 1,775 passengers (535 first class, 550 cabin class, 690 tourist class).]

Raffaello

Although the planners at first intended that the *Raffaello* and *Michelangelo* would have black hulls, the ships were painted all-white. Their most distinguishing feature was their birdcage-like, lattice funnels (*above*). The two ships were soon instantly recognizable for this feature. Because the funnels were placed rather aft than was usual on such large liners, they were capped by two long, black deflectors to keep smoke and soot off the aft passenger decks.

The *Michelangelo* arrived first, in May 1965, followed by the *Raffaello*, shown preparing to leave on her maiden voyage from Genoa in July (*opposite, top*). [Built by Cantieri Riuniti dell'Adriatico, Monfalcone, Italy, 1965. 45,933 gross tons; 902 feet long; 102 feet wide. Steam turbines, twin screw. Service speed 26.5 knots. 1,775 passengers (535 first class, 550 cabin class, 690 tourist class).]

The *Michelangelo*, shown passing lower Manhattan on August 4, 1965 (*opposite, bottom*), and the *Raffaello* were certainly the biggest, fastest, and most lavish liners to serve the postwar Mediterranean trade. They ran a balanced express run between Naples, Genoa, Cannes, Gibraltar, and New York. Occasionally, these schedules were extended to include Casablanca, Tenerife, Lisbon, Barcelona, Palermo, and Palma de Majorca. These longer sailings had special appeal as round-trip cruises and were advertised as "Mediterranean Go-Rounds."

The Italian Superliners

122   *The Italian Superliners*

Aside from their financial troubles, the sister ships had some other problems. The *Raffaello*, shown departing from Genoa *(opposite, top)*, had a rather serious engine room fire on October 31, 1965, and then in May 1970 collided with a tanker in Algeciras Bay. Probably the most serious incident was the lashing of the mighty *Michelangelo* by the severe Atlantic storm of April 1966 *(opposite, bottom)*. The aluminum fore structure crumbled under the extreme pressure of one giant wave, and it was only by pure luck that the entire bridge did not collapse *(above)*. While most passengers had been evacuated from the forward section of the ship, one couple refused to move. They were lost, swept into the sea. Days later, the *Michelangelo* arrived at New York, hours late and with large canvas coverings across her forward decks. Afterward, in repairs at Genoa, both liners had their support structures changed to steel.

The first-class ballroom aboard the *Raffaello* (***above***) was dominated by great crystal chandeliers. The first-class hall aboard the *Michelangelo* (***left***) was the perfect entrance to a modern liner, a city at sea, a floating luxury hotel. The theater aboard the *Michelangelo* (***below***) was among the largest afloat in the 1960s.

All Italian liners had a well-appointed chapel, and the *Raffaello* (***opposite, top***) was no exception. A first-class suite (***opposite, middle***) was priced at $1,500 per person for a peak summer season sailing for seven days from New York to Naples aboard the *Raffaello* in 1965. A first-class twin-bedded room (***opposite, bottom***) aboard the *Michelangelo* cost $700 per person, also in 1965 and also for the seven-day crossing.

124

125

The *Michelangelo* and the *Raffaello* (**above**) were "warm-weather ships" and were rightfully known for their vast outdoor decks.

By the late sixties, with fewer and fewer Atlantic passengers, the twin superliners were sent on more frequent cruises: to the Caribbean, to Carnival in Rio, around the Mediterranean. However, their range was limited by their great size. Often, they had to anchor offshore because of unsuitable docking facilities. In this winter view at New York in January 1969, three Italian liners are in port at the same time (**opposite, top**). The *Michelangelo* is just docking while the *Raffaello* (right) and the *Leonardo da Vinci* are at berth, at Piers 90 and 92. To the far left is the *Empress of Canada* of Canadian Pacific.

The operations of the *Michelangelo* (**opposite, bottom**) and the *Raffaello* were complicated even further by frequent, often unpredictable strikes and job actions by the Italian crews. Delays and even canceled sailings became commonplace. The ships often sailed from New York and Genoa days off their published schedules.

126 *The Italian Superliners*

The Italian Superliners 127

In the face of embarrassing losses, the Italian government finally cut the subsidies to the two big liners and later to the entire Italian Line passenger fleet. The *Raffaello* made her final departure from New York in April 1975 *(above)*, the *Michelangelo* less than three months later. Both ships were kept at Genoa at first and then, in September, laid up at La Spezia. All of their furniture and artworks were removed, and nets were placed over the swimming pools. Only caretakers visited thereafter. The Iranian government under the Shah bought them in 1977. They were delivered by way of the Suez Canal, manned by Italian crews of about fifty each. They were intended for use as military barracks. The *Michelangelo* was moored at Bandar Abbas, and the *Raffaello* was at Bushire. But they soon fell into poor states—neglected, sun-scorched, rat-infested. The *Raffaello* was destroyed in February 1983, during an Iraqi bombing raid. She remains submerged in harbor waters.

The *Michelangelo* was sold to Pakistani scrappers in the summer of 1991 and towed to Gadani Beach for breaking up. It took six months to demolish her, and she yielded $1 million in scrap metal. This view *(below)* dates from November 9, 1991. Her parts are scattered on the beach, and the last remains of her once impeccable hull sit in the background.

Costa Classica

For the next two decades the Italians seemed to lose interest in building large passenger liners. But as the international cruise business expanded, especially in North America, and as Italian shipyards regrouped under the Fincantieri, orders began to flow in. Up until the late 1980s, the Finns, the French, and even the West Germans had secured most cruise ship orders. But the Italians were supported by enthusiastic and generous support from the Italian government (with construction subsidies of as much as 50 percent). In a short time over a dozen ships of 50,000 tons and more were in construction. Among these were two sister ships for Costa Cruises, the *Costa Classica* (**above**) and the *Costa Romantica*. In the early '90s, they were part of Costa's $1 billion fleet renewal and expansion. These ships now spend their summers in the Mediterranean and winters in the Caribbean. [Built by Fincantieri shipyards, Venice, Italy, 1993. 53,700 gross tons; 723 feet long; 98 feet wide. Diesels, twin screw. Service speed 20 knots. 1,905 maximum cruise passengers.]

The Italian Superliners

Carnival Destiny

The Italians built new ships for Princess Cruises, luxury cruise yachts for the likes of the Renaissance and Silversea cruise lines, the first for a series for the newly formed Disney Cruise Lines, as many as seven luxury ships for Holland America Line, as well as some of the largest passenger vessels ever conceived. When the 101,000-ton *Carnival Destiny* (*above*) was delivered to Miami-based Carnival Cruise Lines in the fall of 1996, she was the largest liner of all time. In the spring of 1998, that record passed to another Fincantieri-built ship, the 109,000-ton *Grand Princess*, part of the British-owned, Los Angeles-based Princess Cruises. In addition, the Italians were fulfilling orders for as many as a dozen more mega-cruise ships. Although the Italian Line is gone, the grand tradition of Italian-built ocean liners continues. [Built by Fincantieri shipyards, Monfalcone, Italy, 1996. 101,353 gross tons; 893 feet long; 116 feet wide. Diesels, twin screw. Service speed 21 knots. 3,399 maximum cruise passengers.]

Bibliography

Bonsor, N.R.P. *North Atlantic Seaway*. Prescot, Lancashire: T. Stephenson & Sons Limited, 1955.

———, *South Atlantic Seaway*. Jersey, Channel Islands: Brookside Publications, 1983.

Braynard, Frank O. *Lives of the Liners*. New York: Cornell Maritime Press, 1947.

Braynard, Frank O., and William H. Miller. *Fifty Famous Liners*, Vols. 1–3. Cambridge, England: Patrick Stephens Limited, 1982–87.

Charles, Roland W. *Troopships of World War II*. Washington, DC: The Army Transportation Association, 1947.

Crowdy, Michael, ed. *Marine News*. Kendal, Cumbria: World Ship Society, 1965–97.

Devol, George, ed. *Ocean & Cruise News*. Stamford, Connecticut: World Ocean & Cruise Society, 1980–97.

Dunn, Laurence. *Passenger Liners*. Southampton, England: Adlard Coles Limited, 1961.

———, *Passenger Liners*. Rev. ed. Southampton, England: Adlard Coles Limited, 1965.

Eisele, Peter, and William Rau, eds. *Steamboat Bill*. New York: Steamship Historical Society of America Inc., 1965–97.

Eliseo, Maurizio. *Rex*. Parma, Italy: Ermanno Albertelli Editore, 1992.

Kludas, Arnold. *Great Passenger Ships of the World*. Vols. 1–5. Cambridge, England: Patrick Stephens Limited, 1972–76.

———, *Great Passenger Ships of the World*. Vol. 6. Cambridge, England: Patrick Stephens Limited, 1986.

———, *Great Passenger Ships of the World Today*. Sparkford, England: Patrick Stephens Limited, 1992.

———, *Great Passenger Ships of the World*. Rev. ed. Hamburg: Koehlers Verlagsgesellschaft mbH, 1997.

Miller, William H. *The Last Atlantic Liners*. London: Conway Maritime Press Limited, 1985.

———, *The Last Blue Water Liners*. London: Conway Maritime Press Limited, 1986.

———, *Passenger Liners Italian Style*. London: Carmania Press, 1996.

Official Steamship Guide. New York: Transportation Guides Inc., 1937–63.

Ships and Sailing. Milwaukee, Wisconsin: Kalmbach Publishing Company, 1950–60.

Smith, Eugene W. *Passenger Ships of the World Past and Present*. Boston: George H. Dean Company, 1963.

Towline. New York: Moran Towing & Transportation Company, 1950–97.

Via Port. New York: Port Authority of New York & New Jersey, 1955–95.

Index of Ships Illustrated

Amerigo Vespucci, 73
Anastasis, 87
Andrea Doria, 99–103, 104, 105, 106, 107
Anna C., 96
Antoniotto Usodimare, 71
Aquitania, 19
Asian Princess, 82
Atlanta, 34
Atlantic, 114–115
Augustus, 16, 18, 78, 79, 80, 82
Aurelia, 94
Ausonia, 90
Australia, 84, 86

Bianco C., 96
Bremen, 19

Caribia, 64–65
Carnival Destiny, 130
Castel Felice, 93
Colombo, 33, 34
Conte Biacamano, 9, 13, 65, 66–67, 69, 70
Conte di Savoia, 47–59
Conte Grande, 10, 11, 12, 13, 57, 67, 68, 70, 107
Conte Rosso, 3
Conte Verde, 2, 3, 4
Costa Classica, 129
Cristoforo Colombo, 106–110

Donizetti, 86
Duilio, 5, 6, 7, 8

Empress of Canada, 127
Esperia, 32
Esquilina, 57
Eugenio C., 97

Federico C., 96
France, 114–115
Frances Y Slanger, 61

Galileo Galilei, 88, 89

Giulio Cesare, 8, 75, 76, 77, 81, 82, 107
Great Sea, 82
Guglielmo Marconi, 88, 89, 90

Hermitage, 65
Homeric, 91

Independence, 104, 114–115

Leonardo da Vinci, 111–117
Liberté, 104

Mauretania, 104
Michelangelo, 119, 121, 122, 123, 124, 125, 127, 128
Monarch of Bermuda, 19

Neptunia, 28, 29, 85
Normandie, 19

Oceania, 27, 28, 29
Oceanic, 92
Olympia, 114–115

Queen Elizabeth, 104
Queen Mary, 114–115

Raffaello, 120, 121, 122, 124, 125, 126. 127, 128
Rex, 8, 36–46, 57,
Roma, 8, 15, 17, 19

Saturnia, 22, 23, 24, 25, 62, 63
Sebastiano Caboto, 72
Southern Prince, 19
Stockholm, 106
Sydney, 95

United States, 104

Victoria, 31, 87
Virgilio, 30
Vulcania, 21, 25, 61, 63, 64–65